HAT

Art Deco version of Mercury (the Roman name for Hermes) in his magic hat, 1933, portrayed in bas-relief at the Rockefeller Center in New York.

These three examples have deep roots in the past and yet are active in culture, referenced often, and easily recognized. Why are they so appealing? They remain key, not only to the way in which people relate to clothing but in the way that culture perceives power, because the transformative nature of the hat is a concept so embedded in most cultures and so entrenched in human consciousness that it has never lost relevance. The hat has always been endowed with an ability to impart properties to its wearer and then to be emblematic of what that signifies. How unusual, and far-reaching, this supernatural role is.

As an object, the hat is made from all types of material, synthetic or natural, is flexible or stiff and appears in all sizes ranging from tiny to big, wide to tall. It suits all heads, adorning babies and adults, and can be stunning in its idiosyncrasy (couture hat) or either reassuring (clan hat) or terrifying (helmet) in its uniformity. Enduring as well as ephemeral, it is handed down through generations, as a crown or an embroidered coif would be, or discarded after a few minutes, as a paper party hat is. But the hat is not only a thing that sits on the head. It is a complex signifier of human consciousness, representing intricate meanings about beliefs that underlie politics, philosophy, language, religion and manners as well as meanings around intimate subjects such as sexuality and identity. A hat can also convey innuendo, satire and inside commentary on any of these aspects of the social imagination.

A presence in society for thousands and thousands of years, the hat is the only, or at least the earliest known, garment depicted in the Ice Age, appearing as early as 30,000 BCE. But its importance can be hinted at far earlier through the carved and drawn abstract forms – the circle, triangle and square – that materialize during the early signs of human life, some as old as 700,000 BCE. There is a potential connection between these linear

The square-shaped mortarboard is associated with balance and judgement.

The conical witch's hat.

The matador's montera is shaped to reference the bull's head.

opposite
The fourteenth-century European butterfly hennin has two horns, often draped with veils.

The Korean *gat* can be tiered and horned.

structures and the tangible hat because hat silhouettes, in general, lean towards basic geometric forms. The square scholar's mortarboard, triangular witch's cone, circular skullcap and cylindrical fez are well known. Many hats, across the globe, appear in iterations of their prototypical shapes, often repeating their initial shape for millennia. Most hats develop from these base forms with additions such as a flap, a protrusion or another geometric form. For example, the European medieval jester's hat adds two horn shapes to a conical cap much as the Spanish matador's hat does to a pillbox shape. The Korean *gat* can appear as horned tiers on a similar pillbox form, made in stiff black diaphanous mesh. The dramatic Flemish fifteenth-century butterfly hennin, with two winged wires draped by veils, also bears some resemblance to the horned skullcap. It is arguable that these familiar geometrical millinery foundations have roots in the abstract drawings of the Ice Age, which in turn can represent the gestations of human abstract thinking.

The hat and its recurrent ancient shapes have evolved into a vehicle for such thinking as still today the hat can confer rank and identity as well as protect, transform, bless, sanction and more. The ordinary hat, once placed upon the head, often becomes a version of the magic hat. It too confers powers. It ushers in supernal worlds. It acts with agency. The Nigerian *ade*, the French crown and the Egyptian *pschent*, all merely hats, become the activation of sovereignty when lifted onto a head in a coronation ceremony. The Shinto *tate-eboshi* and Catholic mitre become signs of divine stewardship when worn by a priest, and the Mayan headdress a conduit to the spirit world. The *kufi*, *yarmulke* and *zucchetto*, all skullcaps, designate and express three different faiths when worn, respectively, by Muslim, Jewish and Christian men. The helmet, of any nation, even on its own, can inspire fear.

The Nigerian *ade* is conceived as a crown that connects the king with his community and ancestors. Its strings are meant to obscure the face and thus indicate the king as a leader rather than an individual.

The crown that French general Napoleon Bonaparte
wore for his coronation as emperor in 1804.

The triangular Christian mitre.

The ancient Egyptian god Horus depicted wearing the *pschent*, a hat that joins the two crowns of Upper and Lower Egypt.

A stela bas-relief from the 8th-century Mayan city of Yaxchilan, Mexico, depicting a ruler wearing an elaborate headdress appropriate for a rite of personal blood-letting through which access to the spirit world was gained.

Japanese Shinto priests wearing the *tate-eboshi* at a ceremony inaugurating a sumo wrestling tournament.

The Head and the Hat

The mundane hat's occult talent occurs, in some sense, because the hat is an article of dress. Unlike clothes, the hat doesn't cover the body but rather sits above it. It has a special relationship with the area of the body that it touches – the head. In many ways, the hat and the head are viewed as a kind of unit. The glove and hand, shoe and foot, shirt and chest, gown and torso, trouser and leg, coat and back, bra and breast or sleeve and arm don't elicit the notion of a 'relationship' in the way that the hat and the head do.

It is obvious why the head is given greater status than other body parts. It is indispensable! Even the heart can be transplanted but the head cannot. It is beautiful, sensuous, versatile. Topped with much-prized hair, the head synthesizes, processes and thinks as well as tastes, touches, smells, hears and sees. It perceives spiritual dimensions and can translate the natural world into abstract renditions. It is understandable that the hat, from its earliest origins, was construed as an extension of the multi-tasking head. Sitting prominently on top of the body, the hat indicates who the person beneath is and signals the identity of that person in either an individual or a social role. As such, the hat represents profound cultural concepts and acts to protect, hold and promote those concepts in a proactive manner. The hat is not static. It is an agent of connectivity.

The hat has been linked in multiple ways with the head's prodigious creativity – at times directly, at times indirectly. Fables and myths about magical hats abound, replete with references to the hat's ability to bring the wearer knowledge and awareness of other worlds. This energized hat-and-head symbiosis appears in concepts of leadership, one that is well illustrated by the *ade*, the Nigerian crown, an object representing the philosophy of the northern Yoruba, dating back to the seventeenth century. The Yoruba view the corporeal head as having a metaphysical head within it, known as the *ori inu*. The *ori inu* navigates between a person and their destiny. This concept of destiny manifests in the king as the head of his population. In the Yoruba community, it is the king's crown, the *ade oba* – a beaded conical hat with long, dangling beaded strings all around its rim – that, once placed on his head, activates the king's personal *ori inu* and, thus, the king's place in the ancestral world. The hat is a conduit between the living leader, his community, the *ori inu* and the lineage of ancestors. The dangling strings, through which the king looks, indicate that the king as a leader is not an individual man. The strings mark that his selfhood is obscured because he is now the generic representative of the ancestors and the community.

The Hat as a Thing

The hat belongs to the taxonomies of both clothing and ritual. As a dress accessory, it is an important and often revered adornment, and as a metonymic object it carries such clout that it has wielded, throughout history, almost unparalleled iconic status. It stands for religion, for governance, for militia, for custom, for tradition, for beliefs, for trade, for clan, for fashion and for entertainment. This combination sets the hat apart from its category as 'dress' (such as a physical crown) or its category as 'object' (such as a symbolic crown). In the hat, they often merge. The hat's role as a symbol is indisputable. It defines core parts of society. Its beauty is irrefutable. It attracts and dazzles. Its practicality is undeniable. It warms, cools and protects and can even be upended and used to carry. The hat is not simply a piece of clothing or simply a symbolic thing. How did such a practical item become one that also conveyed status and identity? When does the hat, as a wearable piece of clothing, begin? When does it appear as functional and when as symbolic? How did the hat become a ritualized object? What did the hat's earliest manifestations mean?

a previous mode. The constancy of these iterations shows that, because it has been afforded such iconicity, the hat maintains stability even through extreme shifts in politics or trends.

Today, men and women still play out statements through their hats. The current coded use of the hat reveals how much this practice is loved and needed. Once it became common attire, the baseball cap was worn to announce a sense of self. It was placed with the visor sideways, backwards or forwards, or with the crown tilted, perched or set back, all at varying degrees – each variation having a specific interrelated meaning. The height of the crown or the width of the brim and accessories such as bands, feathers or diamanté implied how the hat should be read. These codes were meant for those in the know.

By the beginning of the 2000s, all kinds of hats had exploded on to the scene as everyday wear. Vogues for men and women soared again as the trilby, Kangol bucket hat, newsboy cap, slouch knit cap, driving cap, cartwheel, beret, Panama and fedora became so popular that even high-end luxury brands such as Hermès and Prada sold costly couture versions. By the mid-2010s, hats were everywhere. They dominated couture, catwalks, celebrity looks, magazine covers, 'cosplay' and gaming. Homemade hats became exciting, and independent hat shops selling sophisticated hats were suddenly common. Masquerade, with a huge emphasis on headgear, became one of the unique marks of the era's zeitgeist. The couture milliner rose to be a superstar.

The hat lives on in the twenty-first century and it is virtually as strong in society as it ever was. Its constant presence reveals how much even the industrialized world, having once cast off the hat, still relies on the hat for symbolism, messaging, beauty, camaraderie, security and transformation.

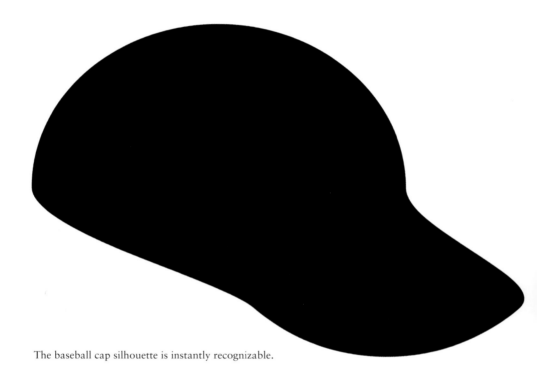

The baseball cap silhouette is instantly recognizable.

ORIGINS / FORMS

You have a head. That is all that matters.
CRISTÓBAL BALENCIAGA, couturier, milliner[1]

The hat is, first and foremost, a form. It is a structured object, one that is, commonly, a particular and recognizable shape that is repeated for centuries. The fedora and top hat, for example, are classified easily by their outlines alone. Hats that have symbolic weight as an identifier, such as an *ade* or crown, display a cultural idea that may be obvious as a social reality (a leader) but ineffable as a concept (kingship). The hat as an objectified thing can become a symbolic form, a visual shorthand used to simplify what could otherwise be inexpressible. Symbolic forms are some of the first human inventions, appearing at least as early as 100,000 BCE, in a period known in archaeology as the Creative Explosion.[2] Hats are known to have existed some 30,000 years ago, in the form of skullcaps and coifs (a small, close-fitting, rounded-square hood shape), and were important enough to be carved on the heads of tiny Palaeolithic female figurines that were otherwise unclothed. It is possible, given the symbolic meanings that hats have always carried, that the hat, appearing in the Palaeolithic Ice Age as a formal sign for an idea, emerged out of the inventive conception of 'form' as a key to thinking. The value placed on the hat, in the origins of human civilization, is revealed in the fact that it is the earliest (as yet) known article of clothing to have been represented in the Palaeolithic era.[3] This was the beginning of the hat's use as a creative 'form' which was viewed as having transformative qualities.

HAT

The skullcap is the first representation of a hat. Carved into a mammoth-ivory figurine from Kostenki, Siberia (in modern-day Russia) and dated to around 30,000 BCE in the Palaeolithic Gravettian era, a skullcap sits on the head of an accurately realized, voluptuous female figure.[4] She wears a necklace or decorative harness that laces over her breasts and behind her back. Her skullcap is fashioned with a series of small, vertical strokes cut into a bowl shape that has a distinct hemline.[5] The head, unlike the realistic body, is only a round ball and the face is a flat slope and has no features of any kind. A compellingly similar type of skullcap appears in Austria, thousands of years later, on a female limestone figure which has been dated to around 28,000–25,000 BCE. This skullcap, also placed on a featureless, ball-like head, is carved in a bas-relief featuring symmetrical rows of what look to be bumps set in a seven-layered coil pattern, which starts at the top and seems to spiral around the head, ending with two extra, shorter, layers at the back. This figurine, known as the Woman of Willendorf, who, like the Kostenki figure, is standing, is one of the most famous Palaeolithic figures.[6] She, similarly, is small (approximately 11.4 cm/4½ in.), has a fat, voluptuous figure, carved very realistically with dexterity and an astute understanding of the body – with one breast slightly larger than the other, distinct vaginal lips, one knee fractionally raised, the thighs positioned as if the feet are turned inward slightly (as is found on other such figures) and body weight well proportioned. Typical of these figures, her arms are negligible, almost sticks, the feet are missing (or very tiny) and her head is only a lump, with a flattened face that is featureless – without eyes, mouth or nose.

The Woman of Willendorf's bowed head and obscured face are almost entirely covered by her coiled headgear. What is placed on her head is set at a slight angle, also suggesting a hat and not hair. Its rows of bumps are neat, uniform and seem to end in a hem, and it encompasses the head.[7] Until the 2000s,

The 'Woman of Kostenki', a figurine of a naked woman with a faceless head, made some 30,000 years ago and found in Siberia, wears a large skullcap-shaped hat.

28

most studies of these Ice Age figures ignored the caps, but they became relevant, if not crucial, in new analyses and are viewed as carriers of exceptional information. It has been argued that the Willendorf cap is a soft hat constructed with vertical stem stitches (a sophisticated backstitch) in a radiating pattern.[8] It has also been argued that its meticulously carved interlacings are there to display or instruct a method of expert weaving.[9] Weaving was an advanced Palaeolithic technology – one, as noted by Elizabeth Barber, the eminent authority on prehistoric textiles, that emerged before pottery and perhaps before agricultural and animal cultivation.[10] As such, it is entirely feasible that this is a hat made from some kind of weave formation. This woven construction would be a product of what Barber has termed the String Revolution, the period, beginning around 40,000 BCE, when string and its various offshoots, such as thread, cord and rope, were invented.[11] It is reasonable to think that this headgear might have had a shamanistic function and was designed to signify specific importance and privilege: a role for hats as a conveyor of information and rights that continues today.[12] It is possible that the minimalization of feet implies that the figure did not walk on earth and that this was intended to suggest it was supernatural. The lack of a face with any features suggests something similar – that the figure is there to represent a community, not an individual. This reflects the principle found in the Nigerian *ade*'s strings, which are there to imply an erasure of personality (so that the king represents the community and not himself).

The 'Woman of Willendorf', a figurine of a naked woman with a faceless head, approximately 28,000–25,000 years old and found in Germany, wears a skullcap-shaped hat similar to that worn by the Kostenki figure.

Such figurines' details draw together weaving (industry), shamanism (religion, leadership) and hats (identifiers), underscoring a connection between headgear, formal symbolism, technological skill and sacred/governing activity. What these woven/stitched skullcaps represent is open to interpretation but it poses a riveting possibility, suggesting that the hat is integral to the evolution of culture itself.

Nude figurines wearing coifs, carved from mammoth ivory and dated to about 20,000 BCE, have been found at Mal'ta, in modern-day Russia's freezing Siberia. Like the figures cited above, they are tiny – approximately 10 centimetres (4 in.) high – but, unlike those figurines, their bodies are lanky and thin, vertically shaped and intensely abstracted with almost no female details, except V-lines for a vagina and for breasts. Their only other humanistic details are thin little arms positioned so that their hands clasp together between the breasts. Some Mal'ta figures wear a thick, curved, possibly fur coif that comes together under the chin.[13] The fur coif is a garment meant for an icy climate, yet the figures are otherwise naked. These contradictions suggest that the coif covering takes precedence over other perishable clothing and that it is significant, due to its prominence and because of the anomalous combination of cold climate, nudity and hat wearing. This oddity conveys meaning – even if, as yet, this is unknown. In his analysis of Ice Age cultures, archaeologist John Hoffecker conflates the two elements – symbolic display and technological invention – that occur, as examples, in the figures cited above, finding that both often happen simultaneously.[14] One of the earliest expressions of human existence, dating back to at least 700,000 BCE, is the rendering and symbolic display of geometric forms. Hoffecker argues that these forms signify the appearance of creative abstract thought, noting that the 'appearance of symbols coincides with a transformation in technological skills'. He describes abstract thinking as manifesting in the earliest forms of humans and as having specifically to do with creating a new object. 'With their talent for externalizing mental representations by their hands – first evident among some African hominins by 1.7 million years ago – humans acquired the ability to translate their thoughts into phenotypic form.' According to Hoffecker, they

A female-shaped figurine, approximately 20,000 years old and found at Mal'ta in Siberia, depicts a thin naked woman who wears a coif head covering.

reversed the function of sensory perception by
converting the electro-chemical symbols in the
brain into objects that had no prior existence in
the landscape. At first, the structure of these objects
was simple, but larger brained humans who evolved
roughly 500,000 years ago began to make more
complex, hierarchically structured implements.
The creative potential of the modern mind, evident
in the archaeological record after 100,000 years ago,
removed all practical limits to the complexity of
technology.[15]

Symbolic forms may or may not be utilitarian, but the
geometric form is. Through its use of a single visual congruent
line or multiple lines, arranged in various patterns, it is able to
render the concept of 'concept'. Neolithic culture abounds in
geometric designs and they have been interpreted as so directly
tied to the Palaeolithic that the eras are indivisible, both worlds
using the geometric as a symbolic means to, literally, activate
an object.[16]

Neolithic archaeologist and scholar Marija Gimbutas argues
that these lines represent life energy and that their application
on an object and figure are there to 'invigorate their effective-
ness'.[17] This ability to stimulate, if not generate, is a quality of
the 'line' that continues, uninterrupted, today. In many ways, the
'line' is the prototypal image, the *ur*-image, in history because
the line – specific, graphic, legible – admits a reader of its form
into a world of thought. That line can render an alphabetical
letter (such as A, B, C), number (such as 1, 2, 3) or symbol (such
as a circle). In all three circumstances the line, thus, 'holds' an
idea, and to 'read' its concrete marks opens a gateway into untold
knowledge. Genevieve von Petzinger, who broke new ground in
her analysis of Ice Age markings, posits that geometric Palaeolithic designs are 'meaningful characters' that 'hold the key' to Ice

such as that of ancient Egypt, where he finds this pairing not only a common practice but one that was 'crucial to the high-cultural core of the civilization'.[26]

This can throw light on why emblematic forms have always been associated with ranks, religions, regions, groups, customs, fads and manners. Hats, representing the people and modes within these kinds of categories, seem to reflect the value placed on early visual geometries because hats are primarily built on scales around the circle, square and triangle and their three-dimensional versions. In these shapes, hats represent multiple social categories and carry intense subtexts, often filled with complex, even inchoate, ideas.

The primal skullcap remains a common hat and is often given great significance, as is its heir, the pillbox. Many hats, such as the bowler and the baseball cap, have radiated out from the round-form skullcap. Headwear such as the hood and bonnet evolved from the coif shape. The imposing, elemental cone appears in the fashion-conscious hennin, occult witch's hat, punishing dunce's cap, ascetic *penitente*'s *capirote* and the menacing Ku Klux Klan hood-hat, to name only a few. Though almost identical in appearance, they have drastically different meanings – illustrated by the idiocy implied in the dunce's cone and the prescience implied in the witch's. The square, as an ideogram, is often associated with balance and thus, at times, with judgement, as demonstrated in the civic square or the four cardinal points. This reveals itself in a hat like the scholar's square mortarboard, the British judge's 'black cap' and the Catholic bishop's biretta. Palaeolithic ideas echo through the meanings applied to the hat's width, length, height and silhouette and arguably underlie the manner in which hats used today can signify intelligence, at some level, via the square mortarboard, or catharsis, conveyed via the *penitente*'s cone.

The hat acts as an intermediary, a three-dimensional version of the geometrically shaped symbol used, in the earliest forms of human thinking, to express ideas. The geometric pattern is at the root of what becomes its three-dimensional version, out of which the hat is built (that is, a circle becomes a sphere, a square becomes a box, a triangle becomes a cone). The form becomes concrete and its progress from a flat line pattern into a solid object evokes the concept of 'process'. A geometric configuration can be seen as a reflection of the *process* of thinking as well as the signification of it. The three-dimensional shape (sphere, box, cone) constructs a structure that is made up of both space (the manifested object) and time (the process of the time passing during a construction that is then inherent in the object).[27] Gimbutas argues cogently that the geometric lines so dominant on Neolithic pottery and figures are renditions of complex philosophical ideas.[28] She perceives in these designs concepts of states of being, such as becoming (as in the birth process), transfiguration (as in the concept of change) and belonging (as in the integrity of a group as a community) – ideas difficult to convey, much less render. The ability to relay concepts that appear in these early lines continue to exist in the hat, as illustrated by headwear like the Nigerian *ade*, which represents (if not incarnates) both leader and community. A group must perceive its own inherent longevity in order to stay intact, and implicit in its affiliations is the sense that the group is always in a state of becoming (unending leadership, unending members) and belonging (unending solidarity). That the hat is a physical rendering of these kinds of key abstract social concepts may reveal how the contradictions of the dunce's, witch's or penitente's cone arise. The cone, as a form, may be there simply to convey both a group's solidarity and its mission. In this sense, the hat acts as a way to render both the individual concept and the process of thinking about that concept.

Thinking Cap

These ideas, which link the Ice Age hat with the action of the intellect, can be found in the concept of the hat as a domain of thought itself, literally as a 'thinking cap'. Traces of the Ice Age hat (as the prototype of the thinking cap) can be found in one hat that appears throughout history – the magic hat, also known as the wishing hat – into which the idea of 'process' as both proactive and procreative is built. This is also a hat that draws together the community, much as the *ade* does, because the magic hat incarnates both the common and the divine. A telling aspect of the magic hat, as a physical thing, is that its form is often mundane, appearing in the shape of a traveller's or labourer's hat such as a cap or a simple fedora. Described as a 'coarse felt hat' in an English play about a wishing hat published at the turn of the seventeenth century,[29] and in a nineteenth-century Grimm's fairy tale as a 'little old worn-out hat' that 'has strange properties',[30] it is similarly defined in many stories.

The magic hat's association with the commonplace has continued into modern times. For example, the top hat used in the magician's show, though linked with the wealthy, was a style worn by many men and women who lived on the lowest rungs of the class system. The *Harry Potter* Sorting Hat, so probing that 'there's nothing hidden in your head / The Sorting Hat can't see', was an old, bent 'pointed wizard's hat' that was 'patched . . . frayed and extremely dirty'.[31] The sacred hat, too, in many cultures has been based, like the magic hat, on the commonplace. This is an important connection as it appears in odd flashes throughout the history of headdresses where hats link invention, knowledge, social structure and sacredness with the mundane. This suggests the possibility that the Ice Age hat was produced as a crucible of the creation of social structures because it links the most common with the most holy/most magical. This hierarchy of the ordinary (labourer) and the sanctified (deity or holy representative), by proxy, reflects all the social structures in between. The magic hat could be said to embody that very conflation.

A cap, as a hat form, is one of the oldest types of headwear. Even the skullcap or 'beret' shape of the Ice Age hat is virtually that of a cap, as it is circular with a soft roomy top into which the head fits. The etymological root of the word 'cap', as Beverly Chico plausibly suggests in her encyclopedia of hats, comes from the Germanic *haet*, meaning 'hut', and is connected to the Belgic Briton word *cappan*, meaning 'wattle huts or cabins'. In these meanings, she sees the cap as a covering akin to architecture.[32] *The Century Dictionary* connects 'cap' to words for cover, such as hood, cowl and the like, but finds the connection to 'hut' uncertain.[33] However, it is not far-fetched that the word 'cap' is about covering (as in its use as the verb 'to cap'). It is a derivative of *cappen*, from which cowl and cloak evolved, and is also connected to the Latin *capere*, meaning 'to take, take in', because it 'envelopes the whole person'. Concealment and deception is also associated with 'cap', evident in its use in nineteenth-century English slang, where it conveyed deceit. To 'set one's cap' meant to 'deceive, beguile or cheat'.[34] This connotation, if not denotation, of 'cap' also occurs in the slang usages of 'bonnet'. In the form of nineteenth-century British street slang known as cant, a bonnet meant a 'gambling cheat or decoy', as well as being simply a stand-in for 'cheating' itself. It was also associated with treasure or money through being used to mean 'bankrupt', because a bankrupt person was made to wear a green bonnet.[35]

The cap that can conceal, beguile or cheat is a recurring feature of the magic hat. One of the earliest known versions is that of the magic felt pileus worn by the ancient Greek god Hermes, which, shaped like a small cone with no brim, was common headgear among working men. Hermes' hat hid him in invisibility and could transport him through flight. A trickster god of theft as well as the deity who took the dead to the underworld, Hermes also represented the arts in invention and literature. He was additionally the patron of travel and so closely associated with it that he later wore a traveller's hat, known as a petasos.[36] His pileus appears in the Homeric epic the *Iliad*, where it was lent to the divine Athene to conceal her in battle.[37] In the *Iliad*, the cap was known as the Cap of Darkness or the Helm of Death,[38] in part because, at that time, it belonged to Hades, the god of the dead, but had been given to him by Hermes. That Hermes was in a position to bestow his pileus on a deity as important as the god of death emphasizes that, of the two gods, Hermes was the older deity.[39] Hermes had an archaic role that has been identified as that of a time figure because he was conceived as a fertility spirit in the millennium before the ninth- or eighth-century BCE era of Homer.[40] In this early form, Hermes drew together the concepts of both life and time into a cycle of birth, decay, death and renewal that occurred within what the ancient Greeks saw as a 'period'. This concept of 'period' was a specific sense of time passing and was measured by the idea of waxing and waning, a kind of measurement more fluid than a time-construction such as 'year'.[41] As such, Hermes is a figure associated with life and temporality. It is important to see that Hermes' magic pileus carries these connotations in antiquity because, though many ancient myths are lost, clues to meaning can be traced through later mythic figures and the physical symbols they carry.[42] The emblematical pileus was worn also as a life symbol by two other early Greek divinities, the male twins Castor and Pollux, known as the Dioscuri, who were born from a single egg and whom Carl Jung construed as time figures, as in ancient myths they were representative of mortality and immortality. Jung further interpreted the twins' purpose – portrayed, as they were, emerging from the life egg – as representing the act of becoming aware when consciousness is raised out of the dark unconscious.[43] This association of the magic hat with time, awareness and consciousness is something that also appears

The archaic Greek god Hermes, trickster and god of invention, literature, travel and time, wears an ordinary hat known as a pileus, but his own hat is magical.

throughout many later tales of the magic hat. These ideas echo the Palaeolithic hat as possibly a manifestation of the concepts of time and process in the act of thinking. This appears even now as the hat as both lived time (worn by a living person) and eternal time (emblem of a social structure). These themes, so strongly imbued in the pileus, reverberate through history in the wishing hat, underscoring the same themes of time, speed, trickery, concealment and knowledge.

The mystic elements that mirror the process of conscious thinking appear in later European stories of a magical hat. In the long, complicated eleventh-century Old Norse *Nibelungenlied* epic, which is based on much older oral tales, there is a magic cap, *tarnhelm* (or cape, the *tarnkappe*), which leads the heroic male, ultimately, to understand secrets of the natural world and comprehend the language of animals. The wishing hat as a version of something magical that opens the door to greater awareness appears again in the sixteenth-century German tale of Fortunatus. Though this story's history is in the oral tradition, its first publication as an anonymous tale has been traced to 1509 in Germany. It became the basis for Thomas Dekker's English play *The Whole History of Fortunatus* (1599) and his later version, *The Pleasant Comedie of Old Fortunatus* (1600). Immensely popular, the story and play were much published, much translated (languages) and much performed, well into the eighteenth century.[44]

The Fortunatus story certainly reflected the burgeoning mercantile world of the sixteenth and seventeenth centuries, because

Castor and Pollux, the ancient Greek twin brothers known as the Dioscuri, who each wore a pileus and were seen as representing mortality and immortality.

it told a morality tale of a poor man who becomes a wealthy merchant, in part through the gift of a magic (ever-filling) purse. He marries, has two sons and builds up a rich trade over the course of his travels, during which he steals the 'Wishing-hat' (from a sultan, signifying that his business extends to the East) and the hat enables him to instantaneously, swiftly fly away. His interest is in money but it is his younger son who, on the verge of his execution, recognizes the Wishing-hat's value. He marvels that the hat offers the truer wealth of knowledge, exclaiming, 'I have . . . knowledge in my Hat' and realizing that the hat could have brought him 'Experience, Learning, Wisdome, Truth'.[45] In Dekker's play the wishing hat is used to transport the wearer. There is a context, however, in which the hat causes those who wear it to experience a broader range of qualities. The 'Wishing-hat' of the play is involved in deceit and transport (Fortunatus steals the hat and zooms off). But the play ultimately reveals the wishing hat to be about offering knowledge and wisdom, which are both, in the tale, tied to the experience of speed, theft and travel.

These same qualities are found in Hermes' magic pileus and, it was been argued, are reflective not of literal travel or treasure but of the process of travelling in thought and the riches of knowledge.[46] They reveal the essence of Hermes as a deity focused on the act of knowing. His divine capacity was to generate and protect invention, literature, thieving, travel, cunning and deception. He also represented the life force and the process of time (as waxing and waning) and in this he was the stable longevity that produced these arts.

Studies of the Fortunatus wishing hat have connected it to Hermes and to his hat's traits of secrecy, rapidity and knowledge.[47] Some scholars have found knowledge to be the covert core of the story and of the hat's abilities.[48] Michael Haldane argues that the Fortunatus wishing hat references the mind itself in its ability to bestow travel and learning.[49] He significantly sees

The merchant Fortunatus steals a magical hat and flies out the window to safety in this illustration of the sixteenth-century tale.

the hat's miraculous capacity to transport as one that ushers the wearer into a deeper awareness of both the outer and inner worlds. He argues that what the hat can do is to 'embod[y] secret or private travel as if the voyager were invisible: the journey of the unseen self'.[50]

These gifts appear in the wishing hat of *The Blue Bird* (1908), by Belgian playwright Maurice Maeterlinck. His play's magical hat offers two children a discovery of the unknown when it opens their consciousnesses by showing them the souls of objects and animals. In the 1918 film version directed by Maurice Tourneur, costume designer Ben Carré created the hat as a beanie with a long pheasant feather. This was a riff on nineteenth-century German walking hats, touching on the wishing hat's archaic fundamentalism (a beanie is a skullcap), its ancient themes of the commoner and travel (it is a peasant hat and a travelling hat) and its modern life (the children's contemporary search)

– all emphasizing how the wishing hat blurs the worlds of the everyday and the preternatural.

These elements of the magic hat as a thing of creativity was fascinatingly posited by the famous collector of fairy tales Jacob Grimm, in his nineteenth-century work on German folklore, *Deutsche Mythologie*.[51] He connected the word 'wish' etymologically with the name of the supreme Nordic deity, Wodan, a god who had a wishing hat that made him invisible, and argued that the words were connected because the divine force in Wodan and the actual forceful act of making a wish were the same thing.[52] Grimm extrapolated on this idea by underscoring that the verb 'to wish' is about an action. The action of wishing is designed to result in making something manifest or causing something to happen. It is an action verb. Grimm underlines that a wish is less about longing than it is about the creation that the wish wills into being. As he puts it, the wish produces the action of a 'melting, moulding, casting, giving, creating, figuring, imaging, thinking faculty, hence imagination, idea, image, figure'. Grimm links 'wish', therefore, with creation and sees 'wish' as a creator just as a god is a creator. He connects it both to personal activation – 'there is about Wish something inward, uttered from within' – and to divinity – 'God imparts wishing.'[53] The idea that the wish (as activated in the wishing hat) is an act of making an image, in effect concretizing a thought or a meaning, draws together the reading of visual language that begins with the Palaeolithic geometric line images with the participation in creative thinking and the hat as magically able to manifest these processes. It connects wish (an act of creation) and the person who is able to acquire learning (create a thought) by the wearing of a hat.

Arguably, these qualities are a representation of the mind itself. The magic hat manifests speed in the same way that the mind does because the hat's talents parallel the speed of thought. The hat opens up new worlds quickly and goes into unheard of (and undiscovered) areas, just as the mind opens up the spatial vastness of the imagination.[54]

This suggests that the wishing hat (magical, useful and common) is an extension of the Ice Age hat – that is, an object that has been made to be a manifestation of abstract thinking. The hat, built upon the concept of geometric forms in the Ice Age, continues into modern times as a magic vessel, imparting knowledge and meaning as if it were a kind of theatrical stage and opening the doors of the mind as if an alphabet waiting to be read. The Palaeolithic graphic geometrical patterns were the beginning of lines that made up alphabetical letters. Through the lines of these letters the mind of the reader is inducted into knowledge as if that reader is flying through the air, as if time-travelling, as if in an out-of-body experience, imperceptible, invisible.

A figure, made in the tenth century CE, of the supreme Nordic god, Wodan (also known as Odin), who wears a pileus-shaped magical hat that gives him invisibility and wisdom.

Like the magic hat, the mind conceals and reveals. It moves with lightning speed and can arrive at another thought or another subject (realm) instantly. It has cunning. It appropriates ideas. It is an unending trove of wisdom. The magic hat enables the wearer to penetrate unseen boundaries, enter into the inner world and supernatural world. It brings freedom from the laws of time and space. It enables the wearer, as a person open to multiple possibilities, to enter the world and see its true structures of the finite and the infinite, and also to enter the self, and find the true self. These are the same qualities that the everyday hat carries. It places the wearer both in a social category – of traditional mores or fashionable modes – and in a private world of self-perception, identifying herself or himself as unique but as part of the larger world.

TWO

SKILL /
THE HATMAKERS

The hat brings the attitude.
PHILIP TREACY, milliner[1]

J ane Loewen's 1926 guide to hat-making, *Millinery*, written for the amateur, illustrates how, even at the level of the beginner, it is skill, acumen, precision, calculation, a sense of space, colour and line harmony (which she calls the 'fundamental principles of line') that are the foundations of a hat. Loewen taps into the archaic formula of the hat's relationship with the geometrical archetype, stressing that millinery is 'an outstanding example of the practical application of geometry', and she evokes the use of *pi* in making the frame and cutting the shape, which are hat-making's foundations.[2] To give the reader scope, she describes the full process used in industry. To start, a wire frame is constructed using exact measurements and bolstered by 'braces' (wires twisted into place to hold the frame tightly). A plaster mould is made of the wire frame, then a wooden mould is created in order to copy the plaster one and finally a steel die is made of the wooden shape. The die forms are used to press wet buckram (a starched cotton or linen scrim) into a crown.[3] The process that Loewen outlines is the basis for almost all hat-making, in some sense, as found in most handmade, ready-to-wear, industrial and couture men's and women's hats. The start of a design shape, the use of a malleable (often organic) material (such as straw, felt or textile) and the need for skill, moulded forms, processes and tools are hat-making's fundamentals. Loewen's story of hat-making moves from the handmade to the industrial, but hat-making's history is much more. It is as

electric with genius, revolution and stardom as it is poisoned with illness, slavery and prejudice.

Millinery, or women's hat-making, has had a long and disjointed, at times spectacular but often difficult, course over many centuries. Men's hat-making, known as hatting, has moved along a more even trajectory. By the Middle Ages, hatting was central to the economy of European daily life, indispensible to the mercantile world as a core driver in small and large economies. Starting as early as the twelfth century and common by the sixteenth, key elements of European hat-making were organized (or amalgamated) into groups known variously as guilds, associations or companies, depending on their status or specificity. The 'Great companies', as they were called, that affected hat-making were groups such as the Mercers (textile merchants), Haberdashers (a fusion of Cappers and Hatters) and Clothworkers. These elite, influential guilds had immense clout in city governance. Others were important 'Minor companies' such as curriers (leather tanners), felters and fullers (felt-makers), croppers (shavers of pelts), dyers and weavers. The assorted groups tightly regulated the quality of materials and the cost of labour, these two aspects of the business being the primary concerns of the industries' laws until the late eighteenth century.[4] These concerns benefited the skilled worker as much as they did the business owner. Workers from these groups, such as felters – always men – had control of the work process as well as the product. They could fit their hours into the trade's demands, and they could determine how many hours were needed to make a product. They were also free to decide how many items they would make in a week. An item's worth was judged by the quality of its material and the skill of its labourers, and the workers were able to negotiate how their labour was determined. Time was a major factor. A single felt hat might take twelve workers nine hours to complete. A collective could refuse to make more than ten hats in a given week, for example.

British advertisement for women's hats sold at Forty Two Hats, South Molton St, London, 1930.

Hatters in the various stages of making men's hats, 1568.

This determination of time as a measure of quality was a sign of the medieval workplace.

The male workers had protection. They had the stability of being part of a company. Laws were in place to keep their premises closed to the unskilled or itinerant and the market closed to inferior materials. Many of these workers acted together as protective collectives, able to bargain with state or city over conflicts. Women had less protection. They worked within a number of textile and clothing industries, but the trades such as sewing and specialities like artificial flower-making and trimming were almost exclusively done by women, often with a mix of skilled and unskilled labour. Because the employees were female and of varied expertise, they were barred from joining major guilds and companies. However, from as early as the twelfth century, women were in some specialized cloth guilds, such as spinning, or were admitted to others. Women dominated silk thread-making and the production of silk, and there were all-female guilds in Italy, France and Britain. Women were also foremost in some decorative manufacturing, such as the making of metallic

A nineteenth-century German hat-maker's coat of arms.

55

thread and ribbons, and, by the seventeenth century, were major controllers in work such as wool dyeing and wool embroidery.[5]

These industries began to change by the end of the eighteenth century, at which time hat-making had settled into the two distinct branches of millinery and hatting, in which men almost exclusively made men's hats and women made women's. Profound modifications entered these crafts, reflective of intense social change in the concept of private and communal ownership and in the expansion of trade. Both industries endured scathing working conditions and both garnered specific reputations that remained part of public perception well into the twentieth century. Hatters worked in a business that had been placed squarely in the economic centre, but from their first collectives to their current unions they have been known for their solidarity and their determination to fight for labour rights.[6] Milliners, as outsiders to the major economies, had to penetrate the system, and though the millinery business came to have great financial successes, it ran into unusual difficulties. Not only was it a lucrative women-run business, it also enjoyed remarkable social power, and these new forces threatened the old establishment structures. A negative reputation formed around the 'milliner' as a type that became virtually mythic, with connotations so broad that 'milliner' (always meaning female) became a term used to define the evils of consumerism, human predation and national ruin.

Existing on the cusp between the Middle Ages and the modern era, the eighteenth-century workplace was affected by the seismic shifts that ran through the global economy during this period – and the artisan workplace and hat-making were affected. Relations between nations and the influence of the powerful textile market (which dominated commerce) were disrupted by the steady rise of inexpensive, internationally traded consumer goods – especially Asian cottons – that began in the late seventeenth century.[7] This rise also brought the influx of new, expanding and gainful businesses such as millinery, opening up an unprecedented area in commerce.

These changes made an impact that was considered revolutionary, creating a 'consumer revolution' virtually as consequential as the industrial revolution of the next century.[8] This consumer revolution was driven by new factors: taste and vogues. It no longer was only about a purchase or sale between buyer and seller. The price was determined by the buyer's tastes. Tastes fluctuated. This indeterminacy became part of the ebb and flow of the market. Such drastic variations in commerce altered long-standing social institutions, based on medieval models, of class, small business and the nature of capital. Hatting was one of the industries hindered by the changes, while millinery was one of the professions that excelled. Hatters had been moving towards what would become a modern industry, with all the necessary foundational roots such as organizations, taxonomies, labour processes, job hierarchies, international commerce and a broad client base. Millinery now had the opportunity to move in the same direction.

Until the eighteenth century, regulatory laws stipulated that hats be made on demand for individual customers. Ready-made items, known as 'stock for sale', existed as early as the fourteenth century in Europe, and men's caps could be found in bulk in some street markets, but the guilds despised these unregulated situations.[9] Ready-mades were also unusual because the fabrication of clothes and their sale were tightly constrained. Sumptuary laws which targeted the sale and purchase of textiles and clothing, as well as controlling what attire was worn in public, were in use in Europe by the twelfth century. The limiting of certain cloths and the regulation of luxury were aimed, in large part, at controlling importation and prices, though what underlay much of this economics was class control of the rich and the poor alike. These laws typically were particular to regions, though there were state sumptuary laws.

An attention-getting hat decorated with vivid ribbons in
Jean-Laurent Mosnier's portrait of a stylish woman, 1790.

Cœffure
à l'Indépendance ou le
Triomphe de la liberté

Paris over rising flour costs, a hat was devised in 1775 as a kind of advertisement and became known as the *bonnet à la révolte* (bonnet of revolt).[47] This 'bonnet', using figures and scripts devised from wire, papier mâché, ribbons and more, signalled a variety of headline events that ranged from the war (the American War of Independence) to the king's health. The eccentricities of the gigantic, modish, lampooning and declarative hat combined a culture of lavish spending with immediacy, communication, defiance and send-up. The hat literally told a story. The person under the hat wanted not just the identification, such as class or taste, that a hat automatically supplied, but to be identified with a full storyline. The late 1770s French hat told such narratives. This means of branding a self with an actual message that was worn on the body was a new twist on the archaic use of the hat to delineate identity. Marie Antoinette adored the *pouf* but used it to political advantage as well, because not only did the *pouf* make the petite queen stand out, giving her height, but she could use its multiple theatrics to convey public statements 'written' into the wig.

Bertin broke the mould for anonymous women in millinery and dressmaking, because she consolidated the business with the performance of the sale and the performance of the style. Her beautiful counter presentations and women-dominated spaces fed the public appetite for a new self-image that was emerging with the consumer vanguard. The eighteenth-century milliner's hat, with its novelty, panache and announcement of self, rushed into the public imagination while the *marchandes de monde* and the entrepreneurial milliner led the way.

The millinery business, as it began to emerge as a profession around women's hats (versus only decorative items) in seventeenth-century Europe and America and one in which women entirely dominated the field, had begun as respectable if not desirable and was one of the leading businesses run by women, often in the top three female professions. It allowed women access to a decent living and became so widespread as to be mainstream. Numerous millineries were run or owned by women by the turn of the twentieth century. Though many were unmarried, some milliners ran large households. Milliners had young female assistants who 'lived in', a not uncommon arrangement, with up to ten girls. They trained girls for this skilled occupation through a seven-year apprenticeship which had roots in medieval systems. In England, the trade was considered a good option for girls and some were sent by affluent parents to live in millinery households as apprentices.[48] Apprenticing poor children, in what were known as pauper apprenticeships, was common. In the American colonies, millinery was considered as solid a livelihood as blacksmithing, and male and female orphans, some as young as seven, were often indentured to milliners. But millinery was also at the hard end of the clothing industry, in both Europe and America. The boutique shops had sweatshop histories, and by the 1800s many milliners slaved for twenty hours a day in dark rooms filled with choking, fibre-packed air.

Making women's hats had four basic steps – designing, constructing a frame, covering the frame and trimming (or decorating) – a process that encompassed various, mostly low-paid, job levels starting with learner, then progressing to improver, preparer, maker, copyist and trimmer. Only a trimmer, who had design skills and was the one who applied the final decorative details, earned a living wage; the others, and those in auxiliary professions such as flower-maker, competed for agonizing seasonal work, during which they laboured around the clock. High seasons lasting five to eight months did not assure a girl of a job as so many were looking for work, and during the slow season she could be jobless for as long as five months.

Women, even when pregnant, laboured in the hard jobs within mining, railroad work, building and the like, but millinery and dressmaking were considered more lethal. In 1843, a British doctor wrote that, as 'corroborated by official authority', there was 'no trade or manufactory . . . to be compared' with millinery and dressmaking as 'no men work so long.'[49] Flower-makers also grew sick from handling the new nineteenth-century bright green dyes, used on stems and leaves, which were derived from arsenic. That women working for starvation wages in these fashion industries used prostitution as a means to survive was public knowledge. A letter from a milliner with a business on London's prestigious Bond Street provoked a front-page editorial in an 1857 issue of the *British Medical Journal* entitled 'Our White Slaves', denouncing millinery as a 'grinding slavery' and the prostitution for which it was 'well known' as worse. New York City records from the nineteenth century recounting the occupations of women arrested for prostitution in one year show that only the numbers for 'servant' and 'tailoress' are higher than 'milliner', but trimmers, straw sewers, artificial florists and cloth-cap makers, all in hat-making occupations, take up much of the rest.

The effects of war, inflation and economic depression, decade by decade, could undercut, at times, even a reliable wage, throwing people into chaotic choices for survival. Prostitution had long been a common recourse for poor women, with relatively minor social negativity as it was accepted that people, women especially, had to find money where they could.[50] The mid-eighteenth-century's desperate Seven Years War that ran from 1756 to 1763, involving Britain, Prussia, Germany, Sweden, Portugal, Spain and Russia, with offshoots in North Africa and British colonies in America and India, had affected many regions, and this, combined with the later turmoil of the French Revolution in the last two decades of the eighteenth century, had multiple repercussions. By the 1790s, a fifth of the French rural population survived by begging.[51] The reality of prostitution as a financial recourse, especially in times when much of the population suffered deprivation, was obscured when late eighteenth-century culture framed prostitution in a very different way. It became part of the breakdown of traditional class divisions, the rise of consumerism and the uneasiness around female entrepreneurship. This made workaday prostitution a catch-all for people's panic about social change. It was identified with profligate sexuality and spending and construed as a vice thought to be destructive to the homeland both economically and morally. Millinery in particular was a prime target. The milliner's large display windows, which had been Bertin's inventive attraction, the preponderance of poor female workers and the dominance of wealthy men among the milliner's clients made millinery the occupation most recognized as concurrent with prostitution, literally and metaphorically.[52]

Though women in many trades were linked with sexual availability, by the eighteenth century, women who ran independent businesses, most specifically milliners and dressmakers, became the focus of slander. In her analysis of the sewing trades, Wendy Gamber notes that this slander was part of 'an index of anxieties concerning women's place'.[53] The milliner's shop, easy for a man to enter and eliminating his exposure at a brothel, was where millinery workers often had sex for pay. The milliner was so associated with sex that the term 'milliner's shop' was nineteenth-century slang for the vagina[54] and 'old hat' for the vagina's pudendum.[55]

The millinery shop came to be seen not just as a business but as a metaphorical 'place' of business. The literal premises became an imaginary 'site' for the conflicted viewpoints in this index of anxieties. By the early nineteenth century, 'public' and 'private' spaces had been gendered – public (such as places of business, governing, entertainment) as male and private (such as the household) as female. However, the many female-run businesses, some of which had been in existence for centuries, muddied the social separation of the two. But it was the milliner's space, public and often financially sustainable, a female one with a known position in the economy, which became a complex trope of this social conundrum. This sense of the millinery 'place' began to mean the actual rooms *and* the profession's abstract position in the economy. Millinery was mixed in with the upheaving transition of the medieval artisan workplace as it was replaced not by a similar form of commerce and labour but by a new form of capitalism.

That these two kinds of millinery places – the literal place and the metaphoric place – were becoming so intensely conflated grew, in part, out of a history of sumptuary laws being used as moral tools. For centuries, excess and luxury had been associated with corruption, and its links to female sexuality already had been exaggerated violently throughout Europe in the sixteenth century with the Reformation's rage against indulgence.[56] Peter Linebaugh points out that at the time of the British Luddite rebellions (starting 1811), when workers such as croppers (who worked in felting), weavers and others smashed the machines that were displacing their hands-on crafts, a cultural mindset was taking shape in which physical space (such as the vanishing artisan's workplace) became a metaphor for changes, especially losses, in long-standing traditions.[57] This sense of a physical space as an imaginary arena, with political and cultural ramifications, was long entrenched in the role assigned to the milliner's shop. A viewpoint that saw women's public premises (or women working in public commerce) as able to debauch women (and, by implication, their male customers) was common and acted as a 'place' where the tensions implicit in consumerism as a vice and a virtue could be enacted.[58]

In his 1872 examination of prostitution, *La Prostitution à Paris et à Londres, 1789–1871*, the Chief of the First Division of the French Prefecture of Police, C. J. Lecour, concluded that 'seamstresses or milliners' ran not a fashion business but rather a 'place of debauchery' that was concealed 'under the pretext of a lucrative business, [where] one takes in young women who will quickly allow themselves to become perverted'.[59] Lecour, as a law enforcer, promoted the centuries-old story that a milliner wasn't working as a milliner, or engaged in an ordinary business in the economy, but rather that millinery hid the female milliner's real intent – which was to corrupt. This positions the millinery 'shop' not as a domain in which ordinary capitalism, as an exchange of money for material goods (ribbons, hats), occurs but is framed as a physical place (brothel) that acts as a symbolic place where capitalism (as a crucial social process) is demeaned and weakened. The milliner's commerce is not viewed as a viable commercial process. Lecour's vision of the fate of the young woman who is drawn into the milliner's shop is that she is no longer a person, one who is starving, seduced or duped, but rather that she becomes 'corruption' itself. She 'quickly allow[s]' herself to 'become perverted'. In this sense, the girl/worker/prostitute is not human but simply a condition.

John Collet's *The Rival Milliners* (1770) depicted millinery as a sexualized business and reflected the prejudices of his time.

The realities of women's work, female workers and their workplaces, and especially of prostitution either as a primary or secondary job, were blurred further in the moralism of the Victorian age, making prostitution either tragic and sacrificing or sickening and predatory – perpetuating a fascination with the woman as 'fallen' that obliterated the horrors of having fallen. This was evident in the *fin de siècle* writers and painters who romanticized and allegorized women's work in the public sphere, a tendency that has been described as 'the strange association of naïve fancies with relentless tragedy'.[60] Sexualized in the arts, politics and social discourse, maids, milliners, farm girls, laundresses and servants appeared not as drudges, but as coquettes in many eighteenth-century paintings and stories. This continued into the nineteenth century with much the same allusions, ending in the sanctified dying 'fallen woman', such as Alexandre Dumas *fils*' famous character Marguerite Gautier in his novel *La Dame aux camélias* (1848), who gives up (and dies without) her lover to spare him from the taint of her courtesan life. Her procurer is a milliner/dressmaker. These conflicted views appeared in the arts especially, promoted by groundbreakers of the day such as Émile Zola and Edgar Degas.

The novelist Zola's focus on the degrading realities of working-class life made him a major figure in literature's naturalism movement but his stories, about sex, poverty and violence, almost never situated his poor women, milliners and washerwomen in any context of actual labour problems or labour protest, even though this was much reported in his time. Zola was drawn to Second Empire issues, especially consumerism, new machinery and urban depersonalization, and he chafed with rage in his 1883 novel, *Au Bonheur des dames* (*The Ladies' Paradise*), about the new phenomenon of the department store. He saw it as nothing less than the dissolution of the 'soul of Paris' and its people. In the way he constructed the story, he revealed the conflicts and prejudices of his time.

Edgar Degas'
ambiguous *At the
Milliner's*, 1881.

Zola's department store, named The Ladies' Paradise, was modelled on Le Bon Marché. In 1852, Aristide Boucicault, a milliner's son, after expanding and innovating the business of what had been a small draper's shop, opened the first department store, Le Bon Marché. By 1887, it occupied a full city block. It is noteworthy that the department store evolved from a draper's shop. Drapers were cloth merchants whose guild was so import-ant that, starting in the Middle Ages, the draper's was considered the premises that most signified the fundamental transactions of commerce, that is, bargaining and payment. In contrast, as part of the eighteenth century's rise in consumerism, millinery premises that sold hats and ornamentation had been deliberately construed by many as a corruption of the clear-cut, direct transactions enacted at the draper's. In the draper's shop, textiles were priced according to measurements of time, based on how long it took to make them. Part of the shift in the eighteenth-century economy – with the flooding in of cheaper imported fabrics and rich, decorative items, merchandise in great demand – had been the movement away from the straightforward, well-established tradition of measuring goods' worth by the labour invested in producing them.

In France, the department store, much as the milliner had been, was both lauded and despised for its promotion of luxury products and a luxe lifestyle. The store's displays, especially its giant windows, were linked to fears that meaningless spending was debasing the economy. Many viewed 'display' as so hypnotic in its effect that a purchase could not be resisted. Just as the Parisian chief of police, Lecour, had insisted that the milliner was about deceit and that her real business (brothel) was hidden 'under the pretext' of her false business (millinery), Zola saw the department store as run surreptitiously by the 'art of hiding'. Denouncing the department store in *Au Bonheur des dames*, he employed the same language as that which had been used by others to denounce the milliner. In his words, the store was described as 'invading, stupid, cunning', using 'snares' and 'seduction' and causing 'fits'. Zola also used the same kinds of words for the store's male owner as were said of the milliner. The owner employed 'tactics' and was often 'amorous', seeking to 'intoxicate' the customer, 'exploit her excitement' and 'trade on her desires' so that she 'could not resist'.[61]

The painter Edgar Degas was also drawn to the milliner and frequently painted her, her shop and her assistants. Today, these pictures are seen as vivacious scenes of young women making, buying or discussing hats, but the nineteenth-century viewer knew that these locations were fraught with contradictory realities. Part of Degas' interest was in the new female shopper, a much discussed topic at the time,[62] but Degas, and other painters attracted to millinery as a subject, knew how millinery stores were perceived publicly.[63] The link between prostitution and the milliner (and other poorly paid female occupations) was openly known and was satirized, sexualized and despaired over, in a range of publications as disparate as cartoons and medical journals. The artists knew that millinery paintings were layered with meaning and that their contemporary viewers did not only see a simple hat shop. They also saw the 'milliner's shop' as the place that originated the slang term for the vagina.

In Degas' lifetime, France had an active population of prostitutes, from the wealthy to the destitute. Up to 15,000 women were officially recorded as being in prostitution in Paris alone between the 1850s and 1870s.[64] That Degas was so attracted to the millinery shops, and was so frequently in them (as opposed to other businesses run by women or other premises, such as brothels, which were overtly sexual), suggests that perhaps he had sex there but, at a deeper level, he and other painters like him shared some identification with the women.[65] Degas' 1881 painting *At the Milliner's*, of two women in a milliner's shop with one woman positioned behind the other, echoes the insinuation of sex so visible in John Collet's 1772 picture of a millinery store. Degas' depiction sexualizes the women's relationship while it occludes the brutality of the milliner's life.[66] This ambivalence reflected that found in the conflicted attitudes about new consumerism. The demonization of millinery as being more about sex than about design, as well as the acceptance of this lucrative trade's contribution to the larger economy, was a microcosm of fears about consumerism's reliance on imports (fashion-driven, feminized, and thus sexualized as voracious) that many felt would ruin the national economy while also boosting it with new taxes and new buyers.

That consumerism was feminized became apparent when the milliner's curse turned into a fascination with and excoriation of the female customer and the beguiling, devilish, irresistible, seductive department store of the late nineteenth century. Labour problems and job conditions were alluded to in some of these narratives but rarely were examined as part of the story. However, women's work and its abuses were on the public radar and many addressed this head on. Rage against expensive fashion and the slave labour that it exploited was an emotion felt by many nineteenth-century European and American progressives, reformers, novelists and journalists, among others, who highlighted rotten working conditions in different ways. Writers such as Elizabeth Stone (*The Young Milliner*, 1843) and Charlotte Elizabeth Tonna (*The Wrongs of Woman*, 1844) attacked the milliners' conditions in plain diatribes and novels. British caricaturist George Cruikshank revealed the reality of women working in the clothing industries with vicious accuracy

George Cruikshank's cartoon *Tremendous Sacrifice!*, 1846, shows the fashion industry as based in the deathly sweatshop labour of women workers.

its profitable exportation made hatting one of the first colonial American industries (and often took the lead[75]) as, unlike other clothing, which relied on imports, hatters had ready supplies,[76] with many hats made from beaver or other fur.

From the eighteenth-century collectives and their struggles onwards, hatters garnered a reputation as staunch fighters for workers' rights. The strategic changes in eighteenth-century artisan customs and the unique stresses in labour relations of the nineteenth century, which continued through the twentieth, involved hatters in landmark labour disputes, strikes and court rulings as well as pioneering work in forming unions and union entitlements. Their legendary persistence, a trait that can be traced back to their collective bargaining tactics of the eighteenth century, gave them a reputation for labour solidarity that outdid all other industries.[77] Striking hatters in the u.s. knew what they were up against as the country had been fraught with violent nationwide strikes through much of the nineteenth century that were met with an equally violent, uncompromising militia. American hatters first staged a strike in 1863 and three years later began to group themselves into 'fair' (meaning unionized) shops within the National Association, though many non-union shops (considered 'foul') continued. In 1884, the United States Wool Hat-finishers Association was formed, and by the early twentieth century this kind of grouping became the norm, where specialist workers linked with a specific type of hat (such as caps) or material (such as wool) amalgamated, much as milliners had done over the centuries. By the 1980s, many hatters, and milliners, had been drawn together under the ilgwu, the International Ladies Garment Workers Union, which had started in the 1910s with the actions of the shirtwaist strikers.[78] This became the most powerful union in the American garment industry and, until the 1970s, one of the most powerful in the country as a whole.[79]

The hatters were behind one of the twentieth century's most important labour cases: a complicated mixture of anti-trust law

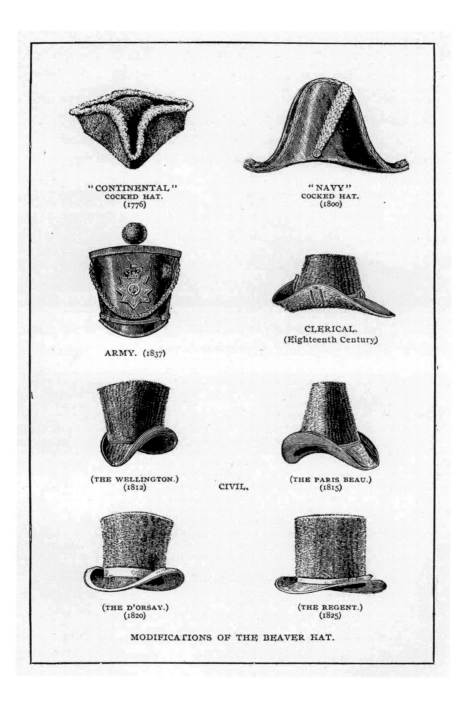

"CONTINENTAL."
COCKED HAT.
(1776)

"NAVY"
COCKED HAT.
(1800)

ARMY. (1837)

CLERICAL.
(Eighteenth Century)

(THE WELLINGTON.)
(1812)

CIVIL.

(THE PARIS BEAU.)
(1815)

(THE D'ORSAY.)
(1820)

(THE REGENT.)
(1825)

MODIFICATIONS OF THE BEAVER HAT.

Some of the many varieties available between 1776 and 1825 of the
practical and beautiful beaver hat.

and union-busting known as the Danbury Hatters' Case or, by its legal title, *Loewe v. Lawlor*. The outcome of this American precedent-setting suit, stretching over fifteen years and heard three times before the Supreme Court, affected labour laws across many trades. In 1902, D. E. Loewe & Company, a non-union fur hat company in Danbury, Connecticut, a major hat-manufacturing centre, sued the hatters' union (The United Hatters of North America) for organizing a strike on its premises. Loewe argued that the 1890 Sherman anti-trust law, which made it illegal to block interstate commerce, indicated that the strike sabotaged his business because, by preventing all sales, it precluded interstate sales. The manipulation of federal law to undermine a strike was a tactic long used in American strike-breaking but this suit went further.[80] It indicted hundreds of union members as well as the union as a whole. They became as equally responsible as the union and would be financially culpable for the fees and penalties if their suit lost. The Supreme Court upheld Loewe's claim, terrifying the union members, who faced steep costs, and setting a precedent that could damage all trades. In the 1930s, the case again went to court and won a ruling that 'labour' was not a commodity and not subject to anti-trust restrictions, showing that the hatters' solidarity still wielded power.

In the early part of the nineteenth century, over a period of less than forty years, machines took over the process of hat-making, allowing the output to increase rapidly. Demand was extreme. Vogues fiercely drove the men's hat market. The light 'silk', as the silk top hat was known, displaced the heavier beaver topper in the early 1830s and the market was swollen by its popularity. In the mid-1860s, top hats were displaced by the 'soft hat', a short crowned, malleable fedora.[81]

The fez had a Western vogue that straddled the eighteenth and nineteenth centuries, and its valuable percentage of the market and multi-level export–import flow were much discussed in the British trade journal the *Hatters' Gazette*. Orientalism had influenced Western fashion for centuries, thanks to a fascination with Chinese aesthetics and Turkish vogues, among others, much eroticized and exoticized by European travellers in Asia and the Middle East, whose accounts of their travels were widely published. Western men had sported forms of turban ever since the medieval chaperon (a large wrapped turban-like hat) crazes, and the late eighteenth-century house turban and house fez, for wearing informally at home, were seen as both practical and stylish. Hats were on men's minds as much as on their heads and, whatever the trend, were much talked about in editorials and bar-rooms. The attention to detail was meticulous. Hat sizes were measured in eighths of an inch and in nineteenth-century England an alarm went up when it was reported, in the *British Medical Journal* and the *Hatters' Gazette*, that head sizes had suddenly diminished, launching into public discourse the troubling question of whether or not this showed a drop in thinking capacity. Hatters were considered central figures. The American Wild West showman Buffalo Bill wrote a 'thank you' note to hat manufacturer E. E. Francis & Co. for the tribute of a hat named after him. The American hatters' trade journal, *The American Hatter*, and Britain's *Hatters' Gazette* illuminated the basic goings-on of the industry but also acted as conversation platforms in which world affairs were commented on in lengthy columns.

Men's hats were as seasonal and as determined by social rules as women's clothing. Boaters were summer wear and bowlers were for autumn and spring.[82] By the nineteenth century, each hat type had multiple variants, at every new season, with constant, infinitesimal alterations to the brim or the crown, as advertisements show.[83] The curled brim became a new feature of hats in 1840 and a craze took off. In a typical advertisement, each bowler of the autumn season of 1894, from a manufacturer like Boston-based Timothy Merritt, would show slight variations in

DEPARTMENT OF
HATS AND CAPS.

MEN'S HATS.

HOW TO MEASURE FOR A HAT

Hat size	Inches around head	Hat size	Inches around head	Hat size	Inches around head
6⅛	19⅜	6¾	21½	7⅜	23⅜
6¼	19½	6⅞	21⅝	7½	23¾
6⅜	20¼	7	22¼	7⅝	24
6½	20¾	7⅛	22½	7¾	24½
6⅝	21	7¼	23		

Men's Sizes are 6¾, 6⅞, 7, 7⅛, 7¼, 7⅜ and 7½. Extra sizes are: 7⅝ to 8. **Boys' Sizes** are 6½, 6⅝, 6¾, 6⅞ and 7. **Children's Sizes**, 6⅛, 6⅜, 6½, 6⅝ and 6¾. **If you do not have a tape measure at hand, use a strip of paper for measuring and attach same to your order.**

Men's Derby or Stiff Hats, $1.50.

No. 33T2010 Young Men's Stiff Hat, in fashionable shape. Is a very neat block, not extreme, but stylish. Crown, 5 inches; brim, 1¾ inches. Fine silk band and binding. Colors, black or brown. Sizes, 6¾ to 7¼.
Price, each.....**$1.50**
If by mail, postage extra, 34 cents.

A Fashionable Block in Men's Stiff Hats for $2.00.

No.33T2014 Young Men's Fashionable Stiff Hat. A strictly correct block in a superior quality. A non-breakable hat that will wear like a $3.00 hat. Crown, 5¼ in.; brim, 1⅞ inches. Fine silk band, binding and sweat. We warrant every hat to give satisfactory service. Sizes, 6¾ to 7½. Colors, black or dark brown.
Each.........**$2.00**
If by mail, postage extra, each, 34 cents.

Late Style and Excellent Value for $2.25.

No.33T2020 Men's Medium Shape Stiff Hat, a little larger than the above styles. Medium curled brim. Not an extreme in any respect, but a strictly stylish block; crown, 5¾ inches; brim, 1⅞ inches. A very fine hat at our low price and we warrant it to give satisfactory wear. Equal to most hats sold at $3.00. Colors, black or dark brown. Sizes, 6¾ to 7⅝.
Price, each......**$2.25**
Postage extra, 34c.

Men's Fashionable Square Crown Hats $2.00.

No. 33T2026 At this price we have the new style square crown hat. A very fashionable block. Crown, 5½ inches; brim, 2 inches wide. A non-breakable hat that will not fail to please in style and quality. Fine silk band and binding. Imported leather sweat-band. Colors, black or dark brown. What size do you wear? Sizes, 6¾ to 7⅝. Price, each..**$2.00**
If by mail, postage extra, 34 cents.

Men's Large or Full Shape Stiff Hats.

No. 33T2040 A style particularly suited to large men. A shapely, staple hat, as shown in illustration. Crown, 5⅛ inches; brim, 2¼ inches. Fine silk band and binding. Sizes, 6¾ to 7⅝. Color, black only.
Each......**$1.50**
If by mail, postage extra, 34 cents.

Our Men's $2.25 Quality Full Shape Hat.

No. 33T2046 Men's Full Shape Hat, same style and dimensions as the above, in the high grade non-breakable stock, with very fine silk band and binding; imported leather sweatband. Color, black only. Sizes, 6¾ to 7¾. Price, each..............**$2.25**
If by mail, postage extra, 34 cents.

Dunlap or Knox Styles.

No. 33T2060 Men's High Grade Stiff Hat, made of very fine quality of fur, with select silk trimmings, in the Dunlap or Knox styles; small, medium or large shape. We furnish the latest styles or shapes as issued in the spring and fall. The usual retail price of this quality is $3.50 and **combines all the points of merit and non-breakableness of the finest derby hat.** Sizes, 6¾ to 7⅝.
Price, each...**$2.75**
If by mail, postage extra, 34 cents.

Fine Wool Fedora.

No. 33T2064 Men's Fine Wool Fedora, medium shape, leather sweatband. An excellent wearing and fine looking hat. Ribbon band, **raw edge brim.** Colors, brown, gray or black. Sizes, 6¾ to 7¼.
Price, each.....**45c**
If by mail, postage extra, 20 cents.

Genuine Saxony Wool Fedora Hats.

No. 33T2066 Men's Highest Grade Genuine Saxony Wool Hat. A shapely hat that will wear in a durable manner, that will please you. **Leather Sweat-band,** and wide ribbon band of good quality, broad brim. Colors, black, brown or gray. Sizes, 6¾ to 7½.
Price, each... ..**75c**
If by mail, postage extra, 20 cents.

Men's Fur Fedora or Alpine Soft Hats.

No. 33T2070 A shapely hat, made to stand the wear. Silk band and binding; good leather sweat-band. Colors, black or brown. Made from nutria fur. Weight, 4 ounces. The sizes run from 6¾ to 7⅝. **What size do you wear?**
Price, each.....**98c**
If by mail, postage extra, 25 cents.

Dressy Fedora Hat for $1.25.

No. 33T2080 Men's Medium Shape Fedora Hat. A quality that is unmatched by any house. Crown, 6 inches; brim, 2¾ inches. A hat very becoming to men of average build. Colors, black, brown, pearl or gray. Sizes, 6¾ to 7⅝. **What size do you wear?**
Each.......**$1.25**
If by mail, postage extra, 25 cents.

Our Trebor Hat, $1.50.

No. 33T2090 We continue to maintain the same grade of fine stock in our Trebor quality as in previous seasons. Made of fine clear nutria fur stock, fine silk band and binding and imported leather sweatband. If not equal to any hat you can buy at home for $2.00, return to us and we refund your money. Crown, 5¾ inches; brim, 2½ inches, of shapely medium curl. Colors, black, brown or pearl. Sizes, 6¾ to 7⅝. Price, each....................**$1.50**
If by mail, postage extra, 25 cents.

Special Soft Hat.

No. 33T2092 Men's New Style Soft Fur Hat with high open curled brim similar to the alpine or fedora style. Crown, 5¾ inches; brim, 2¼ inches. The stylish and proper hat for young men and at the same time not too extreme. You will pay $2.00 at retail for a hat no better than we send you for $1.50. Fine silk band and binding. Colors, black, steel or pearl. Sizes, 6¾ to 7⅝.
Price, each...... **$1.50**
If by mail, postage extra, 25 cents.

Our Special Soft Hat.

Full Shape.

No. 33T2094 Men's Full Shape Hat, similar in style to the one above but larger shape. Crown, 6 inches; brim, 2¾ inches. A shape that is particularly desirable for tall or heavy men. The quality we will send you will be found equal to hats retailing for $3.00. Fine nutria fur, fine silk band and binding. High open curled brim, as shown in the illustration. This style will please you. Colors, black or steel. Sizes, 6¾ to 7⅝.
Price, each.... .**$2.25**
If by mail, postage extra, each, 25 cents.

Fine Nutria Fur Fedora Hat for $2.00.

No. 33T2097 The Memphis. Raw Edge Genuine Nutria Fur Fedora. As a late fall and early spring hat this number cannot fail to please. Crown, 5¾ inches; brim, 2⅝ inches. In colors the bands (of gros-grain ribbon), are a shade darker than the body of hat, a contrast that lends beauty to this clean cut hat. Russia leather sweat-band. Colors, fawn, pearl, brown or black. Sizes, 6¾ to 7⅝.
Price, each.. .**$2.00**
If by mail, postage extra, each 25 cents.

An advertisement for men's hats showing the many ways in which a hat type, such as a bowler, could be configured.

beaver was sold to the French as *castor gras* and to the English as 'coat beaver'. But a more intense method was needed and the mercury process, called carroting (because of its reddish colour), became the standard. *Alice's Adventures in Wonderland's* illustrator, John Tenniel, drew the Mad Hatter as a short man with a very large head, wearing a tall, plump, funnel-shaped beaver top hat. Mercury sickness manifested in tremors, derangement and hostility, and Carroll's Hatter, touchy, shaky, rambling and incoherent, exhibited these signs. Mercury was known to have poisoned substantial percentages of fur-cutters and hatmakers. As late as 1945, the affects were still reported in the workplace. The u.s. public health department described 'chronic mercurialism' as 'characterized by fine intention tremor; psychic irritability of an exaggerated degree; dermographia [skin that grows sensitive to scratching], excessive perspiration, and abnormal readiness to blush; exaggerated tendon reflexes; pallor; and certain abnormalities of the mouth'.[85] Though mercury was banned officially in the United States in the 1940s,[86] the effects of mercury on hatters

Nineteenth-century workers during the production of men's hats using deadly mercury to break down animal fur in the felting process.

were apparent even into the 1960s and men could be seen, in old hat factory towns like Danbury, shaking and raging.[87] Mercury is so toxic that even a modest handling of a nineteenth-century top hat can result in death, and clothing archives continue to keep them wrapped in plastic.

Social Imaginary

Both the professions, millinery and hatting, have been used (and still are) to connote aspects of women and men that belong in the social imaginary. In the history of the two professions, the hat, as always, carries complicated meanings, at times even representing conflicted ideas that the culture finds difficult to convey. It is significant that the hat retains this ability to mean something symbolic, even to relay the most prominent social label given to the imagined female – that is, sexuality – and to the imagined male – that is, authority. By the 2000s, millinery had become a profession for both women and men. But 'hatter' had taken on another new meaning. It

Sir John Tenniel's famous illustration of the Mad Hatter in Lewis Carroll's *Alice's Adventures in Wonderland*.

still connoted maleness, but the word 'hatter' in the 2000s had a connotation of power, in particular male power, seen in a negative context. It became part of twenty-first-century slang and though unspecific it seemed to point to occupations associated with men. A number of uses of 'mad hatter' appeared in various phrases. For example, an unreliable CEO had been designated a 'mad hatter'. Other 'hatter' references include a bad drug high, withdrawal from society, criminality or posturing.[88] This new take on 'hatter' seems to resonate with the 2000s theme of exposing the destructive side of male power as seen in certain prominent social movements such as Me Too and Black Lives Matter. That the hat/hatter is featured in contemporary slang suggests that the concept of the 'hat' still acts as an indicator (or a holding place) of social constructions, social contradictions, social fears and social projections.

Jean Seberg in Jean-Luc Godard's *Breathless* (1960) wearing her boyfriend's fedora with her own sense of style.

THREE

FASHION / LANGUAGE

A hat is a performance.
JUDITH SOLODKIN, milliner[1]

'Fashion is easier to understand than language itself.'[2] With this comment, the Metropolitan Museum of Art's Head Curator of the Costume Institute in New York, Andrew Bolton, underscored that fashion is not a peripheral part of culture. Fashion is core to how a culture functions.[3] Fashion is a lively thing. It not only moves *within* commerce, revolution, class and art, it can be the very force most pushing it. By placing clothing and fashion's changes in clothing in the forefront of social communication, and in bonding the two, Bolton points up that communication is as much read at a visual and visceral level as it is perceived through words. Clothes are deeply felt and all societies use them to express their ideas, laws and beliefs. People identify themselves, consciously or unconsciously, with their wardrobe and it can become, for each person, an emotional milieu, pulling up feelings of sanctuary, solidarity and individuality as well as softening feelings of alienation.

In her analysis of clothing codes, Patrizia Calefato argues that personal clothing is a place of transformation. She takes as an example the protagonist from Marguerite Duras' novel *L'Amante* (The Lover, 1984) – a young girl who, in deciding to wear a man's fedora, feels that she, at last, can 'see myself'. This insight is profound because it transcends the material world and places her not, in her words, in 'nature' but reveals who she is, at the core, in the 'spirit'. She finds the hat not only an exultant expression of her individuality but one that 'completely transforms' her.[4] This illustrates, for Calefato, how, as a person makes choices about how to dress, a style appears that reveals back to the wearer who they are. By the assembly of an outfit or a choice of a hat, to use her example, the person manifests their own identity, visible before their eyes.[5] Once a person has considered their own clothes to be an individual style, that style transforms clothes from mere objects into a means to objectify (and thus make visible) the subjective self.

This echoes the 'wish' as a magical manifestation, a magical act of creation that leads to the act of knowing. Here, in the hat, the girl discovers her heretofore unseen self. In this way the truth about herself is made apparent. This places the ordinary hat (such as the girl's fedora) that magically conjures up a treasure (of self-awareness) for the wearer in the same category as Fortunatus' magic hat and Hermes' enchanted pileus. These hats induct the wearer into self-awareness, through wisdom, and into the riches of exploring both the inner and the outer worlds. Like the abilities of the Dioscuri, symbolic figures of time who wear the magical pileus (as two sides of birth – mortality and immortality), the girl's ordinary fedora also, as Jung postulated, raises awareness (consciousness) from the unknown unconscious. The magic hat plays that part, in so many of its incarnations, of leading the wearer into a bigger world. Maeterlinck's children's hat reveals the secret soul of things. The *Harry Potter* Sorting Hat points the individual to their inner being.

It is telling that Duras chose a hat for her protagonist. Though hats are able to conjure a unique self to the wearer, they have another quality – that of endurance, much as the magic hat does. This dual nature, of stability and the ephemeral, acts as the background to the nature of society and the discovery of self within society. Diane Crane in her analysis of clothes sees this quality as special to hats, citing them as 'closed texts' because most cultures know them as fixed and constant. Hats are stable to such a degree that Crane regards them as 'universally understood'.[6] They are understood because hats thread all the layers of a social structure, and as such they are familiar and easily read.

Hats are given a complex agenda. They are relied on to express both clear meaning and also meaning that is potentially too dangerous to fully reveal. The hat can be steeped in deadly social connotations, because laws directed at dress often carry fears. These fears are about the weakening of commerce or social structure but, more realistically, they are to do with fear of the power of the public. An enforced wearing, or banning, of items of attire criss-crosses the history of clothing, but laws to do with clothing almost always are broken. Dress is personal, and therefore dress laws, more than other kinds of restrictions, have an ingrained conflict in them – a struggle over asserting the personal identity that people feel is inherent to wearing clothing in the face of regulations preventing them from doing so. However, the conflicts involved in dress codes and sumptuary laws can not only bring out inventiveness, they can bring out self-definition.

For centuries, hats have had a central place in the moral adjudications about how a woman or a man should act. These judgements change constantly. The moral value attached to clothing often emerges out of a chain of events. Hats, as physical items, depend on resources that are accessible. What is available depends on what can be found locally, the cost of labour or the cost of an importation. These costs lead to financial regulation and this in turn produces sumptuary laws. Sumptuary laws are situational and can change quickly or last for decades. Though these laws directly tie to the market, they often are merged with social mores and become rules concerned with propriety. Such rules are frequently imagined to be equal to the legalities that control finance and have the legal rationale of sumptuary laws, but they are actually about controlling people. They 'legislate', at the micro level, the wearing of clothes via rules that are really only opinions, often ones that cloak personal emotions about status or sexual feeling. Rules of propriety always disguise systems of class and slavery. But, unlike other kinds of laws, they always give rise to noncompliance, because people have passions about what they wear. This, in turn, highlights the hierarchies that the law-breakers are defying. This is the ever-shifting milieu in which cultures assign meaning to clothing.

The Banned and the Unruly

Hats are some of the most legislated articles of clothing. They are given roles to play and agendas to enact. To name a few out of millions, some of which are discussed below, hats with agendas are found in every sphere of society. These agendas can either confront social customs or uphold them and appear, to give just some examples, in hats that are sacred, such as the *kufi* and mitre; gang-affiliated, such as the top hat and the cone; those that affront and get in-your-face, such as the fontage and hennin; those made for practicality, such as the newsboy cap and coif; those that are beloved by fashion plates, such as the tricorn and cavalier; and those that are purely symbolic forms, such as the mortarboard and Black Cap.

Though the hat is a critical signifier, perhaps the only other signifier that outdoes it is the bare head. The bare head has been an emotional issue for societies and religions throughout history and hats, remarkably, have been the solution. While the hat only covers the hair, it somehow acts as a panacea for the deeper problem of why a bare head is an issue at all. Perceived as so important that its infraction might result in death, the bare head has been associated with vulnerability and a loosening of social constraints that appear in states of mourning, humility, peril, subjugation and immodesty. These states suggest loss of control and a sense of being overwhelmed, human conditions that can present a threat to social cohesion. In a sense, a bare head has been seen as an individual head, one that is vulnerable and potentially unallied or alone. Because of this the bare head has been viewed as a humiliation and in some cases as a privilege.

The twentieth century brought the bare head into a new realm where it was stripped of its old connotations. By the 1960s, it was viewed as liberating because, possibly, it was a sign of the democratization with which the twentieth century, known as the People's Century, was associated. This was the century in which people's struggles and demonstrations strengthened unions and pushed reform and numerous new civil liberties into law. These phenomena paralleled the gradual shift towards the bare head. The twentieth-century bare head became a place that no longer revealed information. Shorn of the hat, the bare head became a new indexicality. It wasn't just bare. It was 'missing' a hat. As a non-signifier of affiliation, income and class, the bare head was a new way of conceiving society.

But, before the twentieth century, taking the hat on and off the head, throughout history, created offences and fealties that, if infringed, could lead to punishment or ostracism. Women, especially, had to deal with injunctions against either wearing or not wearing a head covering. Men also have been forbidden to go bareheaded in many circumstances that are to do with religious customs, where a hat could not be removed in public.

The enslaved have been one of the most marked of such groups and typically forced to wear a hat or barred from wearing one. In some societies, the enslaved have been forbidden the status of the hat, a custom that has lasted for centuries and has appeared as late as the twentieth century in places like Cameroon.[7] In classical Athens, women and men wore their hair loose and, as a way to set them apart, female slaves, unlike free women, had to crop their hair.[8] Greek slaves wore hats to indicate their enslavement. If they gained liberty (some could buy freedom or have it granted), they were still not allowed full citizenship and could not go bareheaded, which was a citizen's right. In the Roman era, this situation was different. Roman slaves, if freed, automatically became citizens. This may have been a hedge against slave uprisings, not uncommon (and not unsuccessful) in this era, because Rome was a slave society, unable to function without slave labour. In the first century BCE, Italy kept one million slaves, which was one-sixth of their entire population.[9] That a slave could gain citizenship would be a lure to stay within the confines of the state. The brimless felt pileus was a key part of a slave's liberation ritual because, as a common hat of Roman men, it symbolized social acceptance. A manumitted slave's hair was shaved in a temple ceremony and the pileus placed on the head. The shaving was an act of humiliation but the hat[10] was construed as an exchange for the lost hair.[11] A freed slave had to wear the pileus but the privilege of doing so was meant, specifically, to signal equality.[12] The pileus became emblematic of freedom in Rome and subsequently was a symbol for it in later history. In the eighteenth century, during the French Revolution, many revolutionaries wore a *bonnet rouge* (red hat), an unmoulded, brimless, red, cone-shaped hat that was worn with the drooping tip hanging off to the side. After the Revolution, when the red bonnet gained associations as a symbol of liberty, it was modelled on the ancient pileus to show solidarity with slave liberation. However, this French Liberty Cap, as it came to be known, had a shape that was wrongly associated with another hat of antiquity. The outline of the French Liberty Cap mirrored that of the Phrygian cap, a soft, conical hat with a tip that draped forwards, worn by the Phrygians, expert weavers and embroiders who lived in what is

A peasant in his pileus in the first century BCE, a common working man's hat in the ancient world.

One of the eighteenth-century images of Louis XVI being forced by the sans-culottes to wear the French Revolution's red Liberty Cap after his capture in 1792 in Paris.

now Anatolia.[13] This Phrygian silhouette rather than the true pileus cone is still used as a sign for freedom.

Perhaps in keeping with the lack of citizenship that women have endured in numerous societies, they always have been caught up in the bare head/hatted head syndrome. The way women wear their hair and/or reveal it and how they wear headgear have been locked into rules configured around opinions about propriety. As was evident in the merging of millinery, sex and consumerism, women and hats were tied to female sexuality until the twentieth century, when the direct connection finally disappeared. In the ancient world, many women were barred from wearing hats (as different from scarves) because hats, signifying status, were the privilege of men. In numerous societies, women could not wear any kind of moulded or made hat, except in rituals, until the fourth century.[14] In subsequent centuries, laws forced many women to cover their heads and a woman's bare head could be linked, negatively, to her sexuality. Prostitutes, as always, had to put up with much regulation of their clothing, especially their headwear. Sumptuary laws and their rules of propriety controlled many nationalities of female prostitutes by censuring their headgear, often with pointless nitpicking. In the fifteenth century, for example, Italian prostitutes could be made to wear horn-shaped hats (signifying sexual misconduct) to flag up their profession.[15] Some were required to wear a veil, which at one point had to be yellow, although the colour-coding was volatile, switching variously between white and black at the end of the century. In the same century, French prostitutes had to wear striped headgear and could not wear veils. During the sixteenth-century Protestant Reformation, Calvinism had pushed draconian laws against sexual behaviour across Europe. The Catholic Church took up similar persecutions by mid-century, targeting thousands of prostitutes in Italy and France. The priests of the French Inquisition seemed to bind the hat and the crime into one object. In their sadistic executions of sex workers, the condemned women were forced, before drowning, to put on their signature plumed, sugarloaf-shaped hats onto which written condemnations had been pinned.[16]

The connection between hat and propriety that became so enflamed in the intense persecutions of sixteenth-century Europe had some roots in the fourteenth century. One of the most dramatic changes in how the bare head, for women and men, was perceived occurred through the 1300 new French law compelling

the upper class to cover their heads in public.[17] This changed
the concept of the bare head in the social hierarchy. The law's
injunction permanently affected the headgear of the wealthy
and added weight to the concept of the bare head as a sign of
impropriety. People flouted these kinds of injunctions, often
in small but defiant ways – such as the beret worn by German
city women in the 1500s, which deliberately revealed hair. It
was condemned as sexual by governing men, but was exalted
as liberating by the beret wearers.[18]

These restrictions and their refusals lasted for centuries,
well into the twentieth. In Europe and America, especially in
the nineteenth century, a woman who was hatless in public was
judged harshly. Women in this era wore bonnets, which typically
had visors with side panels down to or around the chin. This
made it difficult to see anywhere but straight ahead. A hatless
girl could brazenly look where she liked. This free condition
was taken to signify sexual availability because a woman's bare
head and her freedom of movement were viewed as a kind of
nakedness.[19] But this propriety 'rule' was a cover, as were many
propriety rules. The true threat was her insubordination. This
is what the tough 1830s New York street gang Bowery girls (who
often worked as milliners and flower-makers) did when they
refused to wear hats as a deliberate snub to 'ladyhood' and its
'bourgeois female decorum'.[20]

This underscores how much a person's deeply felt feelings
about clothing can infiltrate the very structures of a society,
structures that are so difficult to oppose that people often are
afraid to defy them. But the seemingly innocuous objects of
clothing are strong motivators and can become disrupters. Being
so personal, clothing can be a conduit through which a person
becomes willing to confront the law and refuse to cooperate. It
is no wonder that the bare head is threatening. It brings with it
a person so undone by pain or so freed by a sense of self that
they perhaps feel who they are, only as individuals, and that they

Caricatures Parisiennes.

LES INVISIBLES EN TÊTE-A-TÊTE

Le Suprême Bon Ton N.º 16.

could, as freewheeling agents, even unwillingly, loosen society's most essential feature – its coherent form. This brings into relief how much attention the hat alone attracts and how much need a culture loads on to it and its ever-lasting essential feature – its coherent form.

Women's bonnets with extreme side panels are sent up in Aaron Martinet's caricature *Les Invisibles en tête à tête*, 1805.

Performance

As milliner Judith Solodkin recognized, a hat is 'a performance'. This performance could be said to be literal because the hat, which staged meaning tens of thousands of years ago, has continued to stage meaning. It is a play understood between the wearer and the onlooker. The hat is arguably the most proactive, even the most animated, of clothes because it can clarify

The *tagulmust*, a turban worn by North African men.

The man's fedora, especially its crisp brim, is often used to suggest an enigmatic, potent masculinity that is associated with film noir.

the senate, who held utmost state power, legislated on where they could be awarded. In some instances, the greenery was cut by the person who wore it, as was customary for young wedding couples, who would wear chaplets (thin, circular ties around the head) of flowers that they had picked themselves.[30] This is a version of hat language, in that the living person is drawn into a relationship with the living hat, becoming a symbiotic pairing. The person who picked the flowers and wove them into a circle is joined with the flower circlet by the act of making it. The pairing is symbolized as a sacrosanct union in the wreath, a union that signals time as both mortal and immortal. The Romans too sensed the life force of that conjoining. The rarest and highest Roman military honour was a wreath made from wild flowers and grass, known as the *corona obsidionalis* or crown of grass, always gathered on a site of a massacre in battle. Living wreaths (made of bay, laurel, oak, myrtle and olive, and each symbolic of a specific achievement) were far more valued than ones made of gold.[31] The use of living material as the highest homage echoes the connection to the life force and the magic hat as argued by Jacob Grimm.

The circle is the base of the skullcap and this hat appears as men's religious wear in the Muslim *kufi* (with various national names), the Judaic *yarmulke* and the Christian *zucchetto*. The pillbox is round and flat-topped and stands as a brimless 5- to 13-centimetre (2–5-in.) crown, making it a raised version of the skullcap. Though the basic form is round, it has numerous variations that include having four squared corners – which can be one of the crown shapes of the hip hop baseball cap, the Catholic bishop's biretta, the Judaic *kepple* and the Chinese Qing Guanmao or mandarin's hat. Its spare, free-standing elegance and simplicity appeals to many. It is the shape of the Muslim man's *taqiyah* (the pillbox version of the *kufi* skullcap), the North African version known as the *chechia* and the nineteenth-century British sailor cap. Its simplicity inspired two fashion revolutionaries of their era. Couturier Paul Poiret favoured the shape in his 1910s high-fashion toque. It remained popular through the 1930s and '40s and was a signature of milliners such as the Parisians Maria Guy and Madame Suzy. In the early 1960s, Halston, the milliner turned couturier, launched his pillbox made famous by Jacqueline Kennedy in 1961. This form returned as a fashion essential in the 2000s.

The plain, circle hat was men's wear in the late sixteenth century, when the taste for an unadorned look flattened European men's headgear into round, pancake-like caps. But by the end of that century, the lavish round cavalier hat, worn by men and women, took centre stage. It emerged into a world marked by the seismic alterations in commerce and employment and the political contentions surrounding them. The wide-brimmed felt cavalier hat had a short crown so that a man could hold the hat under his arm (the women did not remove theirs) in hat honour practices, was typically white or light brown (sometimes

A young Roman poet crowned with a wreath of leaves. In ancient times, the living wreath was one of the highest honours one could receive.

A young man in Kenya wearing a *kufi*, a hat worn by men worldwide, in a pillbox or skullcap form, often for religious or national traditions.

Crewmen in 1945 wearing the classic British sailor hat, a shape that has appeared in fashion trends.

dark) and displayed large, coloured (red, white and blue) plump ostrich plumes in the hatband. It led the fashion. Though it was linked to the Royalist soldiers of Charles I, who fought Oliver Cromwell's Roundheads in the English Civil War (1642–51), the hat was glamorized through the mystique of the Musketeers, guardsmen made famous by French novelist Alexandre Dumas *père* in his 1844 serials and later novels about these soldiers of Louis XIV. The cavalier hat was a seductive answer to the clipped headgear of the previous century and suited the late 1600s style of erotically loosened women's dresses and men's thigh-high boots and ballooning shirts and breeches. Well-to-do women wore their wide-brimmed hats on the side of the head, pinned to their piled-high hairstyles, and men often turned one part of the brim up for extra flourish or fully raised the front.

The felt cavalier was echoed in the nineteenth-century fedora, and the latter's soft but elegant shape conquered the twentieth century. It had a strong medium-sized brim that could shade and keep the wearer dry (unlike the short, tight bowler brim) and, like the cavalier, it was meant to be worn with the brim turned. The fedora was typically styled with the brim down in the front and up in the back, but it could be done in multiple ways. The fedora was de rigueur men's wear from the late 1880s well into the late twentieth century (and reborn in the twenty-first), and by the 1930s it had even dwarfed the popularity of hats like boaters, caps and bowlers. The fedora became a favourite to such a degree that it was worn by virtually all adult men in America and Europe until the late 1960s. There was an air of the distinguished and the artistic in the fedora. Beverly Chico connects its origins to the theatre specifically, citing, as the source, the 1882 play by the ever-well-dressed French playwright Victorien Sardou, *Fédora*, a murderous story of a royal Russian Romanoff, played by superstar Sarah Bernhardt. The play has been cited as one of the 'most successful in the history of theatre',[32] and Bernhardt's performance considered so sublime, as one contemporary extolled, she acted with 'such tigerish passion [that] no one has been able to match it since'.[33] The word 'Fedora', a Russian proper name, had such cachet that when the fedora came on the market at that time, to name it fedora was a luminous association with the play.

The trilby was a version of the fedora but smaller with a short narrow brim. Popular among young men in the twentieth century and popular again among women and men in the twenty-first, the trilby was named after the artistic girl in British

The wide-brimmed eighteenth-century cavalier, a beloved hat
worn with style by men and women.

Oscar Wilde wearing a fedora, 1882.

writer George du Maurier's novel *Trilby* (1895), who lost her mind under the spell of the terrifying hypnotist Svengali. In one of the many dramatic adaptations, Trilby's costume signified her as a Bohemian (a meaning in the nineteenth century that associated artists and nonconformity with Eastern Europe) by dressing her in a small fedora with short brim, turned up at the back, a hat common among Bavarian peasant women.[34]

The common round hats of the sixteenth century were visible again in the widely worn newsboy cap, soft, wide, round, with a minute visor, of the nineteenth and twentieth centuries. But the hat that won the hearts of most of the population, across the classes, was the bowler. The bowler's durable crown initially was made to weather storms and rough riding for men who worked on country estates. Its invention is often attributed to the eighteenth-century British squire Thomas William Coke (grandfather of adventurer Jane Digby) or his brother Edward, but it was, in fact, made for the Cokes by hatters William Bowler and John Bowler in 1850, under a commission by the London hatters of St James Street, Lock & Co.[35] First viewed as a country hat, its round shape and tight upturned brim lent itself to being worn and cocked in numerous fashions, and it quickly became a popular hat for urban life. It was so common that it appeared as far from Britain as Bolivia. Stories vary about its Bolivian origins but the most likely is that it came with nineteenth-century British, bowler-wearing, colonial workers at the start of catastrophic wars in this part of the world between French occupiers and British interlopers. The men were brought to the remote country (so high in the Andes, it has altitudes of 3,800 metres/12,500 feet) to lay railway tracks. Aymara Indian men took up the bowler but later the women claimed it and even appropriated the male custom of taking their hats off in church.[36] The women still wear a grey or brown bowler, at times small, set at a slight angle on the head – and even very young girls wear the hat.

By the 1910s, the bowler's stylish air made it attractive to all types of men for all types of reasons and for every price range, and it was even marketed as the 'headgear of democracy'.[37] The bowler became associated with money once it was part of the uniform look of the British businessman – worn on top of the head as if, sitting squarely on the man himself and on his brain's fiscal acumen, it showed stability. But it was also a common street style and, as an affordable item, was a good hat for a poor man, who could strike an attitude with a cool hard tilt of his bowler. Cinema made it special. Charlie Chaplin was one of the bowler's most famous aficionados. In the late 1890s, when Chaplin began his career on the stages of the British music halls, the bowler was a staple worn by famed performers. But

Bolivian women in their traditional bowler hats, which had been introduced into the country by British colonial rail workers in the nineteenth century.

when he began to act in films, he counted on the hat creating empathy for his film character, the Little Tramp. Chaplin took a few years to create a costume that worked to make the Tramp an everyman visibly down on his luck who wanted more for himself. Chaplin's bowler deliberately conveyed mixed messages. It was slightly too small, worn right on top of his head but with a hint of a tilt. This told the viewer that the Tramp wasn't a sport per se and was even harmless, yet he pined for propriety and to have fun with a girl (a narrative of longing in which the Tramp was usually portrayed). Chaplin's costume of a failed man was so successful that he felt he 'owed everything' to it.[38]

Chaplin made his bowler represent a yearning for virility. The ingenious comics Stan Laurel and Oliver Hardy played a version of the everyman and also used their bowlers as a mark of a kind of asexuality. But in the 1930s, post-Prohibition America embraced it as macho wear for both cop and gangster and, in Germany, the bowler could construe super manliness. The fictional criminal Mack the Knife appears in the 1931 German film *Die 3 Groschen-Oper* (*The Threepenny Opera*) looking directly out from under a well-tilted-down brim, bringing to the bowler an air of aggressive power and rakish virility. The bowler, in the u.s., began to lose its impact in the 1940s and became a sign of the outdated past in city life. However it continued to be commonplace in the UK for almost another three decades. In the late 1970s, American dancer and choreographer Bob Fosse brought the bowler back into cultural consciousness when it became his trademark and part of a new American dance form. Fosse had started using a bowler only by chance because it initially was meant to hide his early baldness. But his choreography embraced a gestural use of the bowler that was both erotic and fastidiously dancelike, with clean, elegant strokes.

Circle / Cylinder

Made of a hard cylindrical crown with a short brim, the top hat appeared under a variety of names with multiple shapes, heights, crowns and brims, in materials of beaver, rabbit, silk, felt, wool, velvet, plush and more, was able to stand, fold and flatten and was purchasable (as new or second-hand) by almost every income bracket. The top hat is all that the name implies. It was the principal male hat for virtually two centuries but it was worn by women too. It was identified as emblematic for bankers, entertainers, street gangs, horse riders, clothes sellers, magicians, cartoon characters and the down-and-out. It signified success among these groups but also was the sign for madness as well as stability and was used to imply both criminality and rectitude.

Beaver fur initially made the top hat the triumph that it was. The animal had been hunted almost to extinction in Europe even through Scandinavia before the fifteenth century because its undercoat mulched extremely well into felt, something that wool and rabbit fur didn't do. But by the late 1500s, as small exports of beaver pelts out of the far northeastern area of the Americas (now Canada) appeared in Europe, a trade started that became part of the massive global trade patterns of the seventeenth and eighteenth centuries that changed the merchant economy.

Invented in the eighteenth century, the top hat rose to glory through the lucrative beaver pelt market, because, as well as its undercoat qualities, its fur felted into a sturdy, glossy substance that could be waterproof. Wool-based felt warped, whereas the beaver hat retained its tough shape.[39] The costly, shiny, rain-dispelling top hat flooded the European and North American markets in the late 1700s and dominated the hat markets around half the globe. Its inauguration threw the top hat into the centre of one of the most profitable trades of the eighteenth and nineteenth century, instrumental in drawing the French, Dutch and British to North America, to deal and fight with each other and with First Nation people. By the early 1800s, the silk top hat took over because it was less expensive once the new trade in cheaper Chinese silk began. It was easier to make and it could be made to collapse, eliminating the stiff top hat's storage problems.

Known also as the stove pipe, the chimney pot, the silk, the topper and the gibus (the collapsible version, invented by the Frenchman Antoine Gibus, in 1840), the top hat's classic incarnations are in black, grey, rust or white colours, with a funnel-shaped or straight cylinder crown and an upturned, curled, flattened or curved brim. The top hat has many associations, but one of its most famous is that of wealth. Rich Uncle Pennybags, the moustached, fat-faced man wearing a top hat and coat tails, is still the emblem for the plutocrat in the Monopoly boardgame and, despite being a look of the past, remains a stand in for 'money'. The top hat's more endearing association is with American dancer Fred Astaire, whose 1930s films almost always featured him dressed in a top hat and tails. One of cinema's great dance sequences, choreographed by Hermes Pan, was in 1935's *Top Hat*, where Astaire dances with men dressed in top hats and tails, whom he eliminates as if they are targets in a fairground shooting gallery by firing at them with his cane.

Despite, or because of, its association with wealth, and because of its classic form and shiny beauty, the top hat has attracted many kinds of people and has become their signature. Magicians took possession of the hat in early nineteenth-century France. That they pulled rabbits out of top hats was an in-joke known to their audiences – the cheaper top hat was felted in rabbit fur. In the 1820s, the Bowery Boys, a young working-class street gang who lived in New York's violent Bowery neighbourhood, adopted the hat. They were some of the first to create a 'look' that emerged from street clothes. They made a gang uniform by rolling up their trousers to expose their black boots, wore red shirts or suspenders, had giant coifed side curls and wore a black tall stovepipe hat. The Bowery girls, defiant in their

"I'M BOUND NOT TO RUN WID DER MACHINE ANY MORE."

F.S.CHANFRAU IN THE CHARACTER OF "MOSE."

As originally written for, and performed by him at the Olympic and Chatham Theatres, New York.

Lith & Published by E.&J. Brown, 14v Fulton S? N.Y.

A member of the mid-nineteenth-century New York gang the Bowery Boys, considered one the first to create a gang 'look' from street clothes.

A second-hand
clothes dealer in
London in 1809.

hatless attire, were as violent as the Boys and many fought in
the gang wars. Some of the most ferocious of the many New
York gangs of that century, the Bowery Boys were organized
and had such great street power, they lasted for decades, well
into the 1860s. Employed (many gangs were not), the Bowery
Boys had incomes but often hired themselves out as thugs for
politicians.

Other gangs also took up the top hat. The Plug Uglies, an 1850s criminal Irish American gang from the East Coast, affiliated with a right-wing political party, wore a funnel-shaped top hat known as a plug. It could be hardened into a helmet by stuffing it with leather and wool and then pulled over the ears in fights. Political cartoonists of the time disparaged the Plug Uglies in their stubby hat in biased, anti-Irish drawings, and their plug became a sign of the criminal. Around the same years, Abraham Lincoln made the common stovepipe his emblem and, with that, gave the top hat an association with honesty. The top hat also acted as the sign of the professional occupation of Christian hat sellers and Jewish second-hand clothing dealers, who travelled and sold wares on the streets.[40] The top hat was a notorious symbol of death and madness because hatters died in droves from mercury poisoning.

In the late nineteenth century, female equestrians adopted the top hat and often became famous public figures. Some of these celebrities came from the circus and some from high society, showing again how the hat crossed class lines. These women sported the top hat with elegance and élan, wearing a style that had a short crown, in white or black, and at times adding a veil that covered the hat and was tied under the chin. Music hall stars of this era such as Vesta Tilley and Hettie King, women who performed their songs dressed as rich men in acts known as 'male impersonations', wore top hats with serious aplomb when playing the man-about-town. In the early twentieth century, black comedian Bert Williams, born in the Bahamas, was

Thomas Nash's bigoted political cartoon *Killing the Goose that Laid the Golden Egg*, 1871, depicting the Irish as criminals by referencing the plug, a kind of top hat worn by the Irish gang the Plug Uglies.

Nineteenth-century women equestrians often wore top hats.

A poster for the Fred Astaire and Ginger Rogers film *Top Hat* (1935).

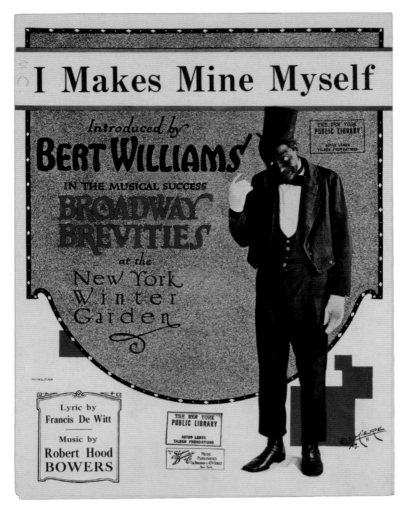

Vaudeville and Ziegfeld Follies comedian Bert Williams in his signature top hat.

a vaudevillian genius who, by 1910, starred with top billing at the Ziegfeld Follies. That he made the top hat his logo had multi-layered significance. In the role of the lowly comic, he wore a well-worn top hat and used the classic comic ploy of wearing undersized clothes. His top hat was slightly too small, telegraphing to the audience that he was down on his luck but felt top drawer. His look was so famous that his slender silhouette cartoon was instantly recognizable.

The top hat has been such a favourite that it has never gone out of style. It was a staple of the twentieth century, often riffing on the meanings established by its older incarnations. Sirens of the 1930s Marlene Dietrich and Josephine Baker acted in the top hat as did numerous actresses, but Dietrich and Baker each put a sexual spin on their version that was so effective their images in the top hat are still very popular. In the 1960s, Dr Seuss's children's book character the Cat in the Hat wore a tall, drooping, striped top hat, characterizing him as an animal imbued with a kind of gravitas (top hat) but one with a weird twist (drooping, stripes). Walt Kelly's long-running 1960s comic strip *Pogo* had an antisocial but endearing and impoverished porcupine character, Porky Pine, who wore a bent, plaid top hat. This identified him with sympathetic caricatures of down-and-out men wearing ragged togs (as seen in performers like Charlie Chaplin and Bert Williams). The 1948 MGM film *Easter Parade* had a dance sequence with Fred Astaire and Judy Garland costumed as down-and-outs wearing bent top hats and singing the ironic 'We're a Couple of Swells'.

The fez is worn, in some variations, throughout the Middle East, Africa and Asia. Its form of a small upside-down bucket, worn by men and women, was a long-lasting vogue in the West, from the eighteenth century into the twentieth. The hat-trade journals discussed it avidly because it was such a reliable sale item and brought a regular income stream.

Triangle

The ancient Egyptians constructed a holy headdress known as the *nemes*. This was a starched rectangle of linen wrapped across the forehead and attached under the back of the head. Its two lengths then fanned out on both sides of the head to form a triangular look. As in so many other sacred/magical coverings, commoners as well as royalty and deities wore it. The countless images that depict ancient Egyptians in this garb show it to have august status. It was the crucial sacred cloth covering over which different Pharaonic crowns and divine crowns were placed. The young New Kingdom pharaoh Tutankhamun was buried with a gold bust of himself wearing a striped (gold and lapis lazuli) *neme*s.

The Christian mitre is made of two curved-edged triangular pieces, usually highly embroidered, that stand front and back to each other so that they can also fold flat together. It originated in various shapes. In the eleventh century, it was worn by the pope as a hard pileus shape.[41] In the twelfth century, it had a conical hood with a forward tip that evolved into two flat triangular shapes each with their edges facing forwards, making the sides appear as horns. It became a simple peaked hood (losing the side horns)[42] and, over the centuries, a hard, jewelled cone in a three-tiered form known as a tiara and similar to the early seventeenth-century Russian tsar's Orthodox crown. Eventually it took on its modern form, returning to the horned cap but reversing the horn shapes from the sides to having them face front and back. The mitre has been linked with the Jewish cantor's *kepple*, which is shaped similarly.

In the late eighteenth century, the triangular tricorn became the beloved hat of Europe and the Americas, worn by men and women. With 'tri' meaning three and 'corn' meaning corner, this was an evenly sided three-cornered hat with, usually, a low upturned brim and crown of the same height and often (unlike the cavalier) in black or darkened colours. It could be small or large and was worn on the top of the head (with the point forward), set on the back of the head (with the central point upward) or rakishly to the side of the head (with the point at an angle). The 'cocked' hat was all the rage and an advertisement would lure a customer by boasting that its hats were 'dressed [decorated] and cock'd' by the 'most fashionable hatters'.[43] Many paintings show young women in masks, veils, laces or hoods

The ancient Egyptian triangular *nemes*, considered sacred, shown here
as Tutankhamun's headpiece.

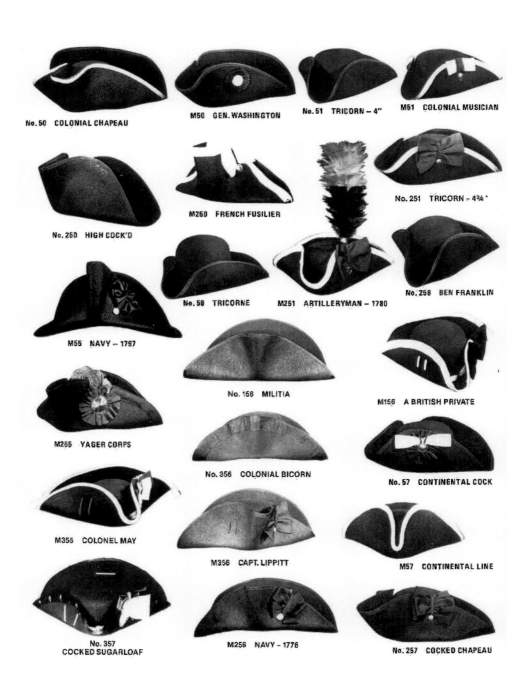

No. 50 COLONIAL CHAPEAU

M50 GEN. WASHINGTON

No. 51 TRICORN – 4"

M51 COLONIAL MUSICIAN

No. 250 HIGH COCK'D

M250 FRENCH FUSILIER

No. 251 TRICORN – 4¾"

No. 58 TRICORNE

M251 ARTILLERYMAN – 1780

No. 258 BEN FRANKLIN

M55 NAVY – 1797

No. 156 MILITIA

M156 A BRITISH PRIVATE

M255 YAGER CORPS

No. 356 COLONIAL BICORN

No. 57 CONTINENTAL COCK

M355 COLONEL MAY

M356 CAPT. LIPPITT

M57 CONTINENTAL LINE

No. 357
COCKED SUGARLOAF

M256 NAVY – 1776

No. 257 COCKED CHAPEAU

A display of multiple kinds of tricorns and bicorns.

A fencer sporting a small bicorn.

wearing a cocked hat as it was popular as an erotic item during the era of the masked ball. Wealthy people, masked and costumed, attended dances at which anonymous sex was, in part, the purpose and in part simply the reputation that these balls garnered. The tricorn was common American gear during the American Revolutionary War and, even now, it remains a patriotic symbol. The military discarded it, at the end of the eighteenth

145

century, in favour of the cylindrical shako, because riflemen found that the tricorn's brim interfered with the action of pulling a gun with a shoulder strap onto the shoulder. Unlike many other hat types, the tricorn did not remain a staple item. By the late 1700s, the top hat swept the tricorn out of fashion and, ultimately, out of sight.

The bicorn, popular in the late eighteenth century and early nineteenth century, was two-cornered, made by drawing up the two sides of a wide brim to form a flat vertical front and back which stood straight up. Defined by this single voluptuous curve, it could be worn with the broad sides facing forwards and backwards or to the sides. It had a distinct look and was only worn by some as an everyday hat but was embraced particularly by the navy, as a sign of the officer. It is most recognized as Napoleonic headgear, worn with flair by Napoleon Bonaparte and his marshals. A version with a shorter front and back was worn in the late 1700s and was notably subscribed to by the French Revolution's *Incroyables*.

Triangle / Cone

The cone is an ancient form, once one of the most sacred single shapes in antiquity, often found as isolated stone forms.[44] One of the earliest was placed at Delphi in Greece, site of the Delphic Oracle, which for generations was considered the *omphalos*, or centre, of the Earth. In the first millennium BCE, the Oracle, always a prophetic woman, was represented by a conical stone. There are two major versions of the conical hat at its most plain. One is the wide cone, very common in the East. The other is the tall cone, a common form in the West. The latter often evokes curiosity because some of its most famous wearers belong to unusual groups such as the Ku Klux Klan, penitentes and witches.

The wide cone is known in Vietnamese as the *nón lá*, meaning 'leaf hat', and the many versions of the Asian conical hat are

Vietnamese food vendors wearing the wide, conical *nón lá*.

found throughout the East, with multiple but slight variations on the basic form of the wide short circular woven cone. It has no brim or crown. Its practicality is legendary as it keeps off sun and rain by entirely protecting the head and face and is a capable carry all, often useful for water as well as objects. A brilliant use of weaving and form, this peasant hat was devised in countries like Japan because labourers were barred from using an umbrella.

The tall cone's long history as a mystical shape has always attracted attention. This shape is found in the hat forms of carnival tricksters and mummers, where it was part of the theatrics that were used either to disrupt social order or to threaten those who disrupted social order. Its cyclone form, as a vortex of energy, is a common thread through some of its most famous incarnations.

The dunce cap is fabled to originate in the thirteenth-century Scottish doctor and alchemist John Duns Scotus's idea that the cone's special abilities could channel intelligence and, as such, he proposed, it was a good object to place on a stupid or unruly person's head. That the witch's pointed cone exists in part because of the reputation of the energized cone cannot be ruled out but, in general, its origins are obscure. Witches have been part of societies for thousands of years. Assyrian ninth-century BCE texts exist that discuss ways to handle witches, men and women who were assumed to harm others by supernatural control and who were seen as threatening to the social order.[45] Centuries later, European witches were seen as similar figures, but their persecution was entwined with intense conflicts during the eleventh-century schism in Christianity, papal struggles, political accusations under the rubric of heresy, and ferocious persecution of Christian splinter groups such as the Cathars and the Vaudois, who were defamed as heretics. Witches, as real or mythic figures, cannot be separated from these persecutions because, in many ways, they were collateral victims of them. It has been well documented that it was within communities living in the Alps and the Pyrenees that the most intense sixteenth-century witch-hunts began. These mountain regions already were associated with the Vaudois and Cathars who had lived in these areas. By the sixteenth century, missionaries had ventured into these mountainous villages for years but found the people difficult to convert. Though they might become Christians, these communities were so isolated that, even if convinced, they easily reverted back to their pre-Christian ideas. It has been argued that the volatility of these peasants' beliefs was exaggerated during this conflicted era and the Church took the opportunity to indict witchcraft – long a vague, marginalized presence in many societies – as an extreme heresy.[46] Witchcraft, under this definition, was turned into an attack on the Church's sense of social cohesion. The association with mountains could

have contributed to the conical hat as a witches' hat because
there is no obvious depiction of the cone hat on witches until
fairly recent times. However, the connection with cone-shaped
hills even appears in Assyrian texts, and here too witches were
described as disruptors of social cohesion and as located in the
mountains.[47] Though there is no direct link between the two
societies, it is not implausible that these ideas could remain in

Jeune fille du Liban coiffée du tentour.
Young girl from Libanon with head-dress.

The tall metal *tantoor* (photographed in 1900), a Middle Eastern hat for women thought to be the inspiration for the medieval European hennin.

folklore traces. The pointed witch's hat does not seem to have existed during the Middle Ages, but it appeared in the late eighteenth century. Francisco Goya's painting *Witches' Flight* of about 1798 depicts three flying Spanish women wearing very tall conical hats. Goya's hats, though, are split at the top, making them look like mitres and suggesting an ironic criticism of Church power. One of the pointed witch hat's most famous renderings was in the 1939 film *The Wizard of Oz*, in which the Wicked Witch of the West wears a wide-brimmed black pointed conical hat, costumed by Adrian.

The hennin was the result of a madcap fifteenth-century fashion for steep, tall conical hats. In the French court, and then across Europe, women sported this startling style, thought to be based on the long, pointed Syrian *tantoor* – a tall, very slender conical metal hat, worn only by women, that had been brought to Europe from the Middle East by the Crusaders. Some hennin were big, built on frames or tiers that might surge almost a metre in the air or, in two-pronged versions, that could be wider than the shoulders. There were tall, fez-like styles with a flat top and many types were draped with veils. Under the hennin were worn wimples – cloth coverings that went under the chin and around the head. The hennin, it has been suggested, was a way for court women to push back against the crushingly male world in which they lived and make themselves demonstrably visible.[48] However, horns and points were popular in this era and at court and appeared in the double-horned jester's cap, in the bycocket (a peaked hat with a long, pointed front as an extension of the brim, worn by men and women) and in the bizarre pointaine, a leather or wooden shoe with a point so long it could stretch as far as 1.25 metres (4 ft) and had to be tied to the leg. Length suited all these extreme sartorial contraptions and it appeared not just in hats and shoes but in long trains and false hanging sleeves.

Another extreme conical hat is the long, sharply pointed, silk-covered headdress known as the *cabriote*, worn by the

Spanish Catholic penitente. These are men who are part of a Catholic movement that began in the sixteenth century, who still walk in street processions today in countries like Spain during Easter, often flagellating themselves as an act of faith and humility. The men want to be anonymous as a show of piety and their hoods are constructed to hide their faces. They wear satin, floor-length robes. This Catholic movement was very strong in the southwestern u.s. by the 1600s and would have had an influence on the American masques and mummers, out of which emerged the cone hat of the American Ku Klux Klan.

The Ku Klux Klan conical hat-hood has roots in American carnivalesque traditions. Often thought to be simply a convenient disguise or created to effect a frightening look, the kkk cone emerged from the white and African American ritual, street theatre, carnival and minstrelsy forms that were strongly established in the States from the seventeenth century and which had been interwoven from Caribbean and European customs. They were almost always accompanied by noise and riotous behaviour. The costumes of these rituals and theatrics were usually composed of a jumble of mismatched clothing, of men wearing women's dresses and of the use of black face. All three together were not uncommon. One of these practices was performed by 'callithumpian' musical bands, made up of young working-class men who, in black face and wearing crazy clothes, enacted a play of – as Dale Cockrell describes it in his detailed study of these dramas – 'communal regulation' known as charivari.[49] Typically at New Year, making deafening noises with drums and whistles, these men would go door to door and harass neighbours, of any class, whom they considered to be weakening their tight-knit community by bad behaviour that ranged from spousal abuse to childlessness. This harassment could be rowdy or could become violent. Cockrell notes that vigilantism, including that of the kkk, was an outcome of charivari, which was considered a male rite of passage and had been part of a long lineage of mob

The conical Ku Klux Klan hat was based in carnival costumes.

Two soldiers in mortal combat both wearing only their padded coifs, known as 'arming caps', typically worn under the helmet in the thirteenth century.

a plain, hard, squarish structure with hood-like contours that gripped the head. It had a stiff, short triangular crown and hard, short sides that were hung with fabric. The gable was worn over a coif and could be jewelled at its edges. This Tudor staple was worn by all English court ladies and remained popular until the late seventeenth century, when it was overtaken by the dramatic flair of the soft, wide cavalier. The gable form resonated in the 1960s in the form of the hip women's helmet hat.

The scholar's square, horizontal mortarboard, attached to a skullcap, is worn to indicate knowledge and education. It is linked to the Catholic biretta, the bishop's skullcap with four

quadrants that either turn the crown into a square or form the whole hat into a square. But the symbolism of the form, as an emblem for the four cardinal points and thus for the stability and authority of knowledge and its breadth across the world, is also a likely source. This sense of judgement and gravitas also appears in the Black Cap, the name for the square-shaped, soft, flat black hat worn by British judges when they pronounced a death sentence.[55]

A nun in the wide headpiece known as a cornette teaching a class in the Netherlands, 1941.

Rectangle

Many singularly unique hats, even rather peculiar ones like the hennin, have launched decades-long trends. The latter half of the seventeenth century in Europe saw one such in the vogue of the fontage: a tall, delicate, rectangular, stacked lace hat with two lace lappets (the long, teardrop-shaped pieces that hang from the neck). The fontage fronted a large hairstyle – a look vehemently derided as indecorous (because it was too high) by Louis XIV.[56] Lace was, until the early twentieth century, a valued creation of skilled intricate work that was so expensive it was a target of theft. Fontage lappets were precious and women were attacked and robbed of them, even while riding in carriages, when thieves would jump on the moving vehicle, reach in through the windows and pull them off.

Another simple form that becomes a unique hat is the side-cap. It is also known as the Gandhi cap because Mahatma Gandhi made it his signature headgear in the 1920s. This is a folded rectangular cloth hat, fastened at both ends, which opens and closes like a single accordion pleat. Gandhi's was always made

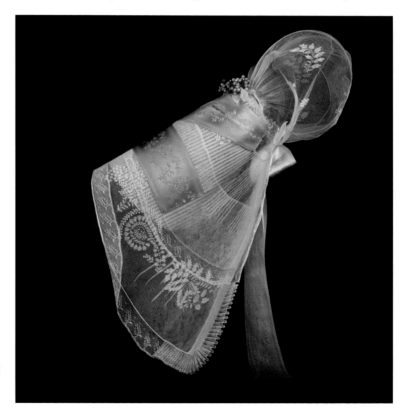

This exquisite traditional bonnet from Normandy is a mid-nineteenth-century Avranches butterfly headdress with embroidered tulle, Valenciennes lace and embroidered stitch, silk brocade ribbon.

from *khadi*, a plain white Indian spun cloth, and he wore it as a show of solidarity with the native industries of India and as a show of resistance to British colonialism. In the late 1940s it also became known as the Nehru cap, once Prime Minister Jawaharlal Nehru wore it regularly, and as an emblem of Indian life. In Asia, many countries have a stiff version of the sidecap, worn by men, such as the Indonesian *peci*. A convenient headpiece, many Second World War servicemen wore a sidecap, which after the war continued to carry the connotation of war-service status. It became the American gas station attendant's hat in the 1940s to give the job a hint of (military) prowess and to promote the

The wildly popular fontage.

rising gas station business. Similarly, a sidecap was (and is) worn by food handlers who are required to cover their hair to ensure good hygiene.

Wrap

The *kufi* pillbox worn by Muslim men can also be bound with a cotton scarf, known as a keffiyeh (among many regional names), to create a turban, one of many connections, historically, between the archaic pillbox and ancient wrapped forms of headwear. One of the world's oldest headdresses, the softly swathed turban scarf is worn across the world by women as well as men, though women do not typically wear the *kufi* under it. The turban, made from a length of cloth wound in such a densely packed way that it becomes hard (and so is legitimately considered a hat and not a scarf), is common headgear of Muslim, Sikh and Hindu men. It became an obsession of the West in the sixteenth century. By the seventeenth century, as the court of Louis XIV welcomed Turkish ambassadors, the Ottoman Empire became a fantasy landscape, appearing as the setting for some of Jean Racine's plays and as part of masquerades and parades. The turban, either with or without the pillbox or fez, was worn, copied and painted.[57] It has never been out of fashion. It was a staple as a women's couture hat throughout the twentieth century and reappeared in the twenty-first.

But the West had, at one time, produced its own version of the turban. The unexpected fourteenth-century French chaperon created a hugely popular vogue that has a special place in fashion. The driving force behind the chaperon's creation was the 1300 French law prohibiting the bare head among the upper class,[58] but it became a progenitor of style, one of the most distinct pieces of clothing to be steered solely by a fashion look. An oddly wrapped form with no religious connotations, the chaperon dominated men's wear in the Middle Ages. Its wide, bulbous,

The fourteenth-century men's chaperon, a style that lasted over
a hundred years.

turban-like form was both wrapped and tied and, at times, had a short curtain on one side and a stringy appendage on the other, in varying lengths, ties and heights. This became a style staple of such importance that it held men's fashion for the entire century and was worn in multiple ways and in multiple fabrics, most commonly silk. By the end of the fourteenth century, the chaperon had swept most of Europe and was so prized that it was a mark of sophistication and wealth for a man to have his portrait painted wearing it. The rich man's chaperon emerged from the prosaic hood, which had been, for centuries, the most common European headgear for women and men of all classes. It is linked in particular with the serf's cowl: a roomy but fitting hood, closed at the throat and draped over the shoulders like a short capelet. During hot weather, the worker would pull up the cowl until the face opening became an edge around the head and tie up the capelet like a turban. When wrapped like this, the cape (known as the patte) and the hood's point, which often ended in a long dangling string known as the cornette or liripipe, would hang down on either side.

South African poet Jessica Mbangeni wearing the African *gele*.

Another extraordinary and stunning version of the wrapped form is the beautiful *gele*, headwear of Nigerian women but popular in many countries. The *gele* is a tied shape more than a wrapped one and dexterity is needed to mould it into a wide, almost bow-like or tall fez form, a composition that has some resonance in the chaperon, in that both are wrapped but neither one is literally a turban. The *gele* has a feel of the turban as its form is created from a single roll of fabric, usually composed of a common African silk-cotton hand-loomed mix, whose slight roughness allows it to be crisply stiff and to hold in place. Also much like the chaperon, the cost of the cloth and its length display the wearer's wealth and status.

that was the most valued. The top milliners prided themselves on designing for the customer. Cristóbal Balenciaga, who designed his own hats, impressed on his clients that a hat was singular to a person and to an outfit. His hats were paired with the ensembles that they were meant for. Lilly Daché, in her memoir, underscored its importance, tying it to a way of life:

> I can make any hat becoming to any woman. But it must be designed for her, and her alone. It must be properly fitted, and it must be in proportion. This, I think, is the secret to success in anything in life.[9]

These talents shaped the consciousness of fashion from the 1910s to the late twentieth century. The milliners were household names. Most were born in the late 1890s or early 1900s and many lived into the twentieth century's last decades. As such, their work and their designer eyes defined that century and set in place many of the ideas that were the groundwork for twenty-first-century millinery's eccentricity, skill and love of the hat's primal forms. The twentieth-century milliners' birth and death dates reveal how linked they are to the nineteenth century and to the twenty-first, which in itself underscores that fashion is never separate in its 'eras' but is deeply interconnected over time.

Millinery was not just an aspect of couture. It was in its very roots. The eighteenth- and nineteenth-century tradition of the dressmaker and milliner as partners meant that the arts evolved together. The influence of one on the other is evident in the careers of some of the most influential twentieth-century couturiers. Many started in millinery. Jeanne Lanvin (1867–1946), Coco Chanel (1883–1971), Charles James (1906–1978) and Halston (1932–1990), as well as film costume designer Gilbert Adrian (1903–1959), all began as milliners. That their century produced some of the bedrock inventions in couture pattern-cutting and the outré has a place in millinery. Knowledge

Young women
in the late 1890s
wearing the
fashionable
pork pie hat.

of hat-making brought a particular set of skills useful to the
sensibility of a dress designer. At base, learning millinery expertise teaches two things: one is the impact of the line and the other
is how to create a structure. A milliner, unlike a hatter, must know
how to make a hat that looks like gossamer but is so secured to
the head that it cannot fall off or blow away. There is genius in
making a solid form appear insubstantial and genius in working
with a fixed object. This skill requires an understanding of form
as a singular entity. A dress's form, even one that is tight, must
include a comprehension of the movement of the body, but a hat
form is about engaging with the immoveable hard head.

The concept of the hat as representing a woman's civil rights
found a new expression at the turn of the twentieth century.
After the 1830s Bowery girls deliberately flaunted their bare
heads as a defiant brand of their strength and solidarity, a new
hat appeared that expressed a similar message. The girls of the
1890s working in factories or entering the office workforce as
secretaries wore the pork pie hat, which was virtually the same

A Léon Bakst costume design, 1911, for Vaslav Nijinsky as Iskender in *La Péri* for the Ballets Russes.

as the men's popular straw boater in shape, though smaller. By 1900, this hat remained the look for these young women and also was taken up by the suffragettes. They were all within the generations of what was called the New Woman and they wore the straw pork pie as an expression of being plain spoken and strong. Another hat worn by the New Woman, from socialites to unionists, was the round tub-like hat known as the 'Merry Widow', popularized by the one worn by actress Lily Elsie in the 1907 play of that name.

Orientalist themes of the nineteenth century continued into the twentieth. The 1910s were rocked by the explosive Ballets Russes, arriving in Paris in 1906 and New York in 1911, with talents that radically changed all their fields. The Russian maestro Serge Diaghilev brought together fabulous Russian-Asian fantasy costumes by Léon Bakst and Alexandre Benois, pounding new syncopations from composers Igor Stravinsky and Arnold Schoenberg, and wild choreography and dancing by Vaslav Nijinsky. At the start of the 1910s, Paul Poiret, the son of French cloth merchants, revolutionized the fashion world. He embraced the Orientalist imagination and the look of the draped body, undoing the tightness of women's clothing by abandoning the corset, returning to the nineteenth-century cut of the empire line (cut just under the bust, leaving the waist free) and introducing harem pants. He brought back the turban and toque. Poiret had an anchor in the august Parisian couturier Jacques Doucet, who clothed aristocrats and costumed the great stage stars Sarah Bernhardt and Cécile Sorel for their theatrical roles. Poiret worked for him in 1896, and the exoticness of this *soigné* atmosphere deeply impressed him as a young man, and he wished 'to be the Doucet of the future'.[10]

The combination of Doucet's clean lines of nineteenth-century elegant excess, the Ballets Russes' futuristic avant-gardism and Poiret's embrace of the archaic form, as seen in his turban and the toque, set the zeitgeist for the twentieth century. Hats were a distinct reflection of this zeitgeist. That the hat and outfit were a unit was something deeply embedded in the couture to come.

A major and perhaps unexpected force in hats in the next decade was in the 'follies'. Much of its impact came from Lucile, the well-known couturière who began her business in London in 1895 with designs so impressive that one writer wrote of her work, 'je vous salute.'[11] Lucile operated couture shops in New York, Chicago, Paris and London. She is credited with transforming fashion shows into events by encouraging her models to be self-possessed young women, proud of their look, much as Rose Bertin had done with her own shop girls.[12] Her work also embraced the entertainments of theatre, cinema and follies. She costumed for the theatre, making a reputation for herself and for then starlet Lily Elsie with her design of Elsie's world-trending 'Merry Widow' hat. Sister to the successful Hollywood screenwriter Elinor Glyn, Lucile was one of the first to dress both the fashionable and the film star and was an important force in the intersections between them. She costumed the stars of that era – Mary Pickford, Pearl White and Gloria Swanson – and also mentored cinema costume designer Howard Greer, who went on to head Paramount's costume department and who hired, and mentored, the legendary designers Travis Banton and Edith Head.

Impresario Florenz Ziegfeld hired Lucile in 1915 to create a look for his prestigious Follies. The Follies were not side entertainments but the start of a new concept in what a show could be. Follies and revues dominated the 1910s, especially in the States, where new entertainment concepts were being built on the tropes of the nineteenth-century musical hall. By the 1920s, these revue shows lined the theatre boulevards of New York, London and Paris and were known for nudity, expensive sets and costumes and a special emphasis on women's headdresses. A music hall/vaudeville format of lowbrow humour, torch songs,

The dresses and turbans of Paul Poiret, illustrated in
1912 by George Barbier for the cover of *Les Modes*.

The actress Lily Elsie wearing the 'Merry Widow', an enormous tub-like hat designed by the couturière Lucile that became de rigueur in the 1910s.

grand tableaux and semi-nude beautiful women framed the acts but it was New York's Ziegfeld Follies, in particular, that created the new paradigm of the showgirl.

These shows were built on the impact of a colossal head-dress. Lucile understood the affect of the 'Air' that Captain Cuthbertson had so exhorted his men to sport. It was about cachet, a cachet associated with manliness but one that was certainly meant to have an erotic tinge. The soldier's hat's dazzling beauty, its almost coquettish toying with the right 'tilt' to augment, if not create, a play for power, easily connected military headgear with the headdress of the star chanteuse and the Follies showgirl of the late nineteenth century and early twentieth century.

The showgirls' stature, glamour and physiques echo that of the bedizened high-hatted military man, whose presentation of self was caught up in what was on the head and how it was worn. The headgear of the European military officers and their fancy uniforms were relatively new, as the regular uniform did not appear in Europe until the eighteenth century.[13] Before that, civilian apparel was common. The uniform sprang into a fashion mode in the early 1800s as a way to lure volunteers into fighting Napoleon's intimidating forces.[14] The uniforms were almost unrivalled in their variety, tailoring, sumptuous material and ornate, complex details of colour, braiding, plumes, tassels, emblems, badges, plates, embroidery, furs, trims, buttons, horsehair, medallions and crests. By 1812, the hats especially grew larger, grander. The crowns towered to 60 centimetres (2 ft). Fur, tassels and plumes were added. Long, freely swinging horsehair tails appeared on the helmets of the French cuirassiers. The white shakos (small cylindrical crowns with short visors) of British officers of the Light Horse Volunteers sported a cockade of plumes centred at the front of the crown that then fell and drooped forward. Russians topped their helmets with 30-centimetre-high (12-in.) double-headed eagles. Nineteenth-century British political cartoonist James Gillray delighted in hiking up the height and width of the militia's looming hats in his lampoons and commentaries on the wars of his era. The military hat styles changed constantly until the First World War's modern warfare, poison gas, trenches and motor vehicles made the cavalry and the splendid military uniform obsolete.

The glamorous regimental hat worn with an 'Air' seemed to reappear on the Follies' stages. The same love of the impact of the giant hat was found in the revue dancer's massive, 2.5-metre (8-ft) spread of a sparkling, fanned-out headdress – a look that had been a hallmark of mesmerizing solo stage acts such as French singer/actress Mistinguett's silk and ostrich-feathered hats, which towered 1.2 metres (4 ft) high when she played revues such as the Casino de Paris.[15] She had followed the wild and impressive nineteenth-century bravura of the singular Gaby Deslys, whose unique style was adored by millions. Cecil Beaton wrote that Deslys cultivated a look and an attitude that 'walked the tight rope of a near-barbarous taste with rare audacity'. The

The ornate, full dress helmet, with a long, sweeping white horsehair plume, worn by the British Life Guards (also known as the Household Cavalry) for ceremonial duty.

In 1933, Paramount's head of costume Travis Banton (possibly with milliner John
Frederics) designed this feathered cloche for Marlene Dietrich in *Shanghai Express*.

Women Holding in Their Arms the Skins of an Orchestra (1936). Historian Alistair O'Neill points out that Legge wore this hat as a performance that deliberately commented on women's rights. Legge saw the vogue hat as a thing that dominated women because women were forced by fashion to submit to wearing one. Legge's version showed the hat, not as something fun or chic, but as an object that 'encumbered and encased'. With this costume performance, in which her head and face were frilled and elided and which she titled 'Surrealist Phantom of Sex Appeal', Legge sardonically reflected on the idea that a woman always had an ever-present, ever-unshakable 'allure'.[23] The 1930s experiments in metaphoric comments, Surrealistic jokes and interpretations of ordinary objects such as those by Schiaparelli and Bes-Ben as the basis for a couture hat returned to the eighteenth-century's poufs, the *bonnet à la révolte* and Bertin's sense of the individual as style.

The 1940s was the peak decade for hats. The stocking cap, the fedora, the fascinator, the draped hood, the sailor and the Breton shapes, as well as the use of long fringes, netted snoods, veils of all kinds and turbans, were all popular. The turban had a heyday. It was much used in France during the war because material was scarce and women would deliberately wind their scarfs high into towering peaks of defiance. In New York, French-born Lilly Daché made her reputation with the turban, a speciality also of John Frederics (who changed his name in 1949 to John P. John and launched his new label, Mr John). Both were two of the most costly milliners, but their work was worshipped and considered the 'benchmark of hat wear'.[24] Daché made the Brazilian actress Carmen Miranda's trademark fruit turban and showered fashion with inventive turban shapes. John had a wild imagination and made extreme – at times, vast – hats with great skill, as well as head-fitting delicate styles. He was known as a master of virtually every kind of hat. The fashion columnist Eugenia Sheppard named him '*the* artist among milliners' and

French-born milliner
Lilly Daché in her
New York studio.

his 1993 obituary in the *New York Times* recognized him as the
Dior of millinery.[25] John also has been credited with introducing
the shoulder bag.

In the Second World War years, the efforts to boost fashion
and millinery were important as the industry was under restrictions. Lilly Daché, John Frederics and Sally Victor formed The
Millinery Fashion Group, a consortium in New York which,
through consolidation, was meant to boost the millinery business.
In 1943, the three milliners were given a Coty, one of fashion's

devastating Korean War of the 1950s didn't want to be associated with the hat-wearing older generation who they felt had led them to death and failure. Hats also needed care, and the 1950s had given rise to 'easy living', a common advertising phrase. Expensive hats were not in the 'easy living' mindset. The most commonly cited cause is that the 1960s focused on democratization and that John Kennedy, known for not wearing the usual fedora, led the way for hatlessness. One reasons was that he had luxurious hair but was a thin man and showing off his hair added youth and virility. It is often mentioned that JFK did not wear a top hat to his 1961 inauguration, as all presidents before him had, but as photographs show, this isn't true. He only removed his top hat for his speech, done by all presidents as a sign of respect.

In the 1960s, many institutions and ideas changed. But that decade embraced Panofsky's recognition of the image as a cultural communication crucial to the structures of society. Canadian philosopher Marshall McLuhan published *Understanding Media: The Extensions of Man* in 1964, stating, 'the medium is the message.'[30] What is read, McLuhan underscored, is not the content but the content's form. That he announced this during the century of the greatest millinery success in history sheds an interesting light on the hat as the enduring vehicle of form and how it has always been, and continues to be, readable as an image.

Hats in the 1960s expressed McLuhan's idea of form in that, when they returned, most returned in primal forms. This latter part of the decade saw the resurgence of the simple line. The hood form, very similar in shape to the original from which fashion once took its hats, the fourteenth-century peasant cowl, became a 1960s icon. Designers Paco Rabanne, Halston, Pierre Cardin and others took up the cowl. They each made a version, commonly known as the helmet hat, of a glamorous stiffened hood, sometimes attached to a dress or coat, that was cut like a hood or a cowl but came together in two solid pieces under the chin. It had the clean lines, shorn surfaces and big outlines that reflected the decade and took the hat towards a uniform, unisex look.

In the late 1970s, Yves Saint Laurent experimented with the Breton, the *nón lá*, the beret, the cloche, the turban, the sidecap, the toque and the mandarin Qing Guanmao. Krizia took up the cloche and the beret. These and the turban appeared in the collections of Biagiotti, Bill Gibbs and Geoffrey Beene. Graham Smith made hats for Jean Muir, favouring the beret form. By the end of the decade, as milliners went out of business, hats were not a constant, but those that were promoted by couture designers were often the beret, fedora and toque. The older hat forms became signatures again. The bowler hat was given a sexual sting when Bob Fosse incorporated it into his erotic, precise choreography and was the key to the enduring image of Liza Minnelli in costume designer Charlotte Flemming's bowler hat, shorts and halter top in Fosse's 1972 *Cabaret*, set in a Berlin club in the 1930s.

The 1980s saw a change in how fashion was perceived. As Olivier Saillard pointed out, this decade brought an 'official recognition of fashion' as it became an integrated part of the larger culture. Venerated museums in the UK, France, the United States and Japan inaugurated well-focused departments of fashion, giving the topic a different kind of gravitas.[31] Ingrid Sischy, editor of *Artforum*, put an Issey Miyake dress on the magazine's 1982 cover, which controversially brought clothes into the realm of art objects, but she stated that the aim was to show fashion as having 'its own systems and languages'.[32] Those systems and languages were strong in hats, and hats, seemingly (to the art world) less controversial subjects, had continued to slip back into the culture as if they had never left. The basic shapes continued to return. The 1980s saw many bare heads, but the simple plate appeared in the fashions of Gianfranco Ferré and the short top hat in those of Perry Ellis. Jean Paul-Gaultier played with the

Pierre Cardin's version of the hip 1960s helmet hat.

Michael Jackson in his signature fedora.

sailor hat. Halston took up the cowboy hat and later so did Ralph Lauren. The cowboy hat look branched out into the next decades and was worn by wealthy women in bright colours, sporting wide brims that rose upward like wings. By the middle of the decade, primal forms had re-emerged as something to work with. Designer Rei Kawakubo, at her company Comme des Garçons, played with the archaic with her twisted and stacked 'paperbag turban' and wave-like conical hat.

Single hats became important as emblems. Michael Jackson took his fedora, designed by legendary Parisian milliner Jean Barthet, as a personal brand logo. How he tilted it far down his head, over his eyes, and how he handled it throughout his performances as he danced became recognized as a silhouette. The headdress of floral ruffles made in the 1930s by British Surrealist Sheila Legge was reimagined by the influential Australian performance artist Leigh Bowery, who died in 1994. His work centred on fashioning his body as a contoured shape inside his tailored costumes that were stuffed and sculpted. He wore a ruffled ball over his entire head in some of his pieces. His designs were extreme versions of ordinary clothes from hat to shoes, and used classic lines to form distinctive silhouettes which were then augmented or expanded. Twenty years later, singer Lady Gaga, an admirer of his work and who had built a look for herself through outrageous outfits (such as her raw meat dress), also took to audacious hats. The massive red hat that she wore on a 2012 *Vanity Fair* cover was credited by her as a homage to Leigh Bowery, mirroring his own take on the grace and swooping shape made by the vertical stance of the wide upright brim of the eighteenth-century cavalier, especially when worn on the side of the head.[33]

In the 1990s, two milliners broke through the taboo of being a 'man milliner' and renewed the status of hats as couture. Stephen Jones studied fashion and had been part of the 1980s London club scene. His talent with the outré, which had a feel of 1930s madcap, made him into a celebrity milliner and he began to set new precedents. Milliner Philip Treacy, younger than Jones, blazed a new trail once his career was mentored by the famed fashionista Isabella Blow, a close friend to couturier Alexander McQueen. She made herself a central fashion figure by creating a distinctive look using hats. Attracted to clothing that repudiated her mother's demand that she demurely represent her aristocratic family by wearing 'nice, simple clothes',[34] she cultivated a look contingent on being seen in extreme headwear, often made by Treacy. She met him when he was still a student at London's Royal College of Art, about to graduate in 1990, and immediately promoted his work. Blow asked him to design her wedding hat as a medieval headdress, and he created a hat that had a small crown but with sides that fitted her head like a helmet. Even then, Treacy's hats were elegantly structured, often with classic, clean, curved lines, but the hats themselves could be extreme. He has worked with large or small hats; ones that form masks or perch precariously on the head. Blow wore these hats as everyday wear, and she courted their look of daring. Treacy's star rose once he produced the hats for John Galliano's seasonal shows and for Karl Lagerfeld, as well as hats for Alexander McQueen and Donna Karan. His clients have ranged from the conservative to the adventurous. His eye has always been attracted to elementary forms. As early as the 1990s, his use of plates, parabolas, spirals and waves, whatever the complication of detail, opened the way for the return of the couture hat.

The joy of the hat marks the twenty-first century and the century is alive with new hatwear. The 2000s saw the return of the mass appeal of every genre of men's hat. The newsboy cap, fedora, panama, trilby, driving cap, Stetson and top hat appeared around the world, worn by both men and women. The love of primal forms, in women's hats especially, was apparent in the vibrant skills of this century's milliners, such as the Romanian Dinu Bodiciu, Australian Dion Lee, French Muriel Nisse,

Contemporary milliner Maiko Takeda's light-catching spiked hat.

Milliner Maor Zabar's whimsical, beautifully structured take
on the Venus flytrap as headwear, 2015.

Men's hats on the catwalk for the 2018 Armani collection.

Milliner Dinu Bodiciu's graceful, mysterious red hat, 2011.

Japanese Maiko Takeda, Israeli Maor Zabar, French Simon Port Jacquemus and American-French Nick Fouquet, to name only a few.

Two ways in which the hat has been used in the 2000s tell much about how it has remained eternal and ceaselessly active in culture. In 2016, artist Nicolás Ortega, illustrating a *New York Times* op-ed by Venezuelan writer Alberto Barrera Tyszka, used hat iconography to suggest a strange conundrum in U.S. politics when it was apparent that the then American presidential candidate, capitalist Donald Trump, resembled in some aspects Venezuela's then president, socialist Hugo Chávez.[35] Trump had appropriated the trucker baseball cap, with a round crown and curved visor, which has associations with the working class, to act as his insignia. He had it dyed bright red and inscribed with the catchphrase 'Make America Great Again'. The illustrator merged the Trump baseball cap with the beret, which is associated with defiance and anti-establishment figures – such as Second World War French Resistance fighters and the revolutionary icon Che Guevara – and is often used as a socialist symbol. This combined hat was the visual most able to sum up the overlaps between the two disparate politicians. The graphic easily showed how the hat was still a potent code and that its instant shorthand effortlessly conveyed meaning built on iconography. The visual impact of hat language was as strong as ever.

In 2018, the floral hat was, as fashion reporter Robin Givhan declared, 'having a moment'.[36] She noted that hats made from real flowers were on the catwalks, particularly those of the designs of the Danish label Noir, whose focus was on natural products and sustainable fashion. It was notable too in the large hat made of live flowers worn by the singer Beyoncé, considered one of the most iconic performers of her generation, when she posed on the 2018 *Vogue* cover for the all-important September issue, which kicks off the fashion season. Beyoncé had thought through what her image could be and, as her personal statement on the *Vogue* issue revealed, the cover shot was, in part, to show her as a person within the continuum of time. She emphasized the present as infused with the joys and hardships of the past and the future, through a focus on self-acceptance, on 'the people who had moved this world forward' and her own ancestry, in which she had traced slavery.[37] Beyoncé's soft, white cotton dress with a loose high collar and ruffled bell sleeves was designed by Gucci but visually alluded to the white dresses of the Caribbean islands as well as the cotton textiles woven and worn by enslaved people in eighteenth-century America.[38] British milliner and florist Phil John Perry created Beyoncé's headdress in a shape that much resembled the copious, asymmetrical African *gele* and he placed this cultural sign in real time because, as he enthused, he 'loved' the flowers' slightly wilting 'tired edge' that revealed their aliveness and transience.[39] Even the look of the photograph felt, as one reviewer described it, as if it was 'in-the-moment'.[40] Through the creative combination of these elements, this 2018 *Vogue* shoot was intended to be, in some sense, a snapshot of the living person in the eternal past, present and future.

These flowering hats, in both of these fashion situations (the *Vogue* cover and the Noir catwalk), were enduring and momentary and, as such, about life and history. They placed

Nicolás Ortega's *New York Times* illustration uses hat iconography to comment on 2016 politics.

The living
green headpiece
is timeless.

the flower hat in a new context. It was not a whimsical hat of
the 1960s, when it had had a brief vogue, but rather one that
referenced deeply serious twenty-first-century issues, such as the
planet's sustainability and the confrontation of historical horror.
There is potential to see these new uses of the live flower hat,
which point to a great solemnity, as a version of the ancient
flower wreath, possibly our first hat, which also pointed to the
important issue of its time, honour.

REFERENCES

INTRODUCTION

1 Stephen Jones, *Hats: An Anthology* (London, 2009), p. 14.
2 Ian Hodder, *Entangled* (London, 2012).
3 *The Merriam-Webster New International Dictionary* (Springfield, MA, 2016).
4 *The Century Dictionary* (London, 1899).
5 Hodder, *Entangled*, p. 42.
6 Josef Svoboda, *The Secret of Theatrical Space*, trans. M. Burian (New York, 2000), p. 8.

ONE
ORIGINS / FORMS

1 Quoted in Colin McDowell, *Hats: Style, Status and Glamour* (New York, 1992), p. 153.
2 Genevieve von Petzinger, *The First Signs: Unlocking the Mysteries of the World's Oldest Symbols* (New York, 2016), p. 3. Petzinger outlines that faint evidence of 'modern thinking' appears 120,000 years ago in Africa in engravings and burial rituals, becoming more apparent 100,000 years ago in a plethora of geometric designs, and 50,000 years ago in 'rock art, figurines, necklaces, complex burials, and music': pp. 59–61; Petzinger notes that 100,000 years ago, people had 'fully symbolic minds like our own'.
3 'Known' refers to what has been discovered to date.
4 Gravettian Period: from around 32,000–29,000 BCE until around 22,000 BCE.
5 Petzinger, *First Signs*, pp. 101, 102.
6 These figures, when first found in the late nineteenth century, were described as 'Venus' figures, as in the 'Venus of Willendorf'. Now they are referred to as 'woman', as in the 'Woman of Willendorf'.
7 J. M. Adovasio, Olga Soffer and Jake Page, *The Invisible Sex: Uncovering True Roles of Women in Pre-history* (Washington, DC, 2007), p. 189.
8 Ibid., p. 185. Adovasio, an authority on textiles and basketry, in identifying these as radial and stem stitches, argues that these stitches

are indications of textile development. A stem stitch is a sophisticated backstitch, associated with embroidery. A radial stitch is one of a series of stitches that all begin at a single point but then radiate out, such as into a fan shape.

9   Ibid., p. 188.
10 E.J.W. Barber, *Prehistoric Textiles: The Development of Cloth in the Neolithic and Bronze Ages with Special Reference to the Aegean* (Princeton, NJ, 1992), p. 4.
11 See Barber, *Prehistoric Textiles*, and Petzinger, *First Signs*, p. 103. String, first made by twisting together short plant strands (such as flax or nettle) to form something inherently strong, allowed humans tremendous leeway in every aspect of life. String tethered animals, tied together bundles, tools, weapons and skins, could create nets (for hammock-sleeping or trapping) and the means to carry, and much more. Threads, known to be at least 36,000 years old, are the basis of clothing and would become the material for the Neolithic loom, which created textiles – one of the world's great industries. In 2013, flax thread fragments were found in Georgia, in Eurasia, showing evidence of having been dyed in pink, blue, black, grey and other colours.
12 Adovasio, Soffer and Page, *The Invisible Sex*, pp. 190, 192. Soffer speculates that the hat designates 'special importance' and 'privilege'.
13 Petzinger, *First Signs*, p. 101.
14 John Hoffecker, *Desolate Landscapes: Ice Age Settlement in Eastern Europe* (New Brunswick, NJ, 2002), p. 1.
15 John Hoffecker, *Landscape of the Mind* (New York, 2011), pp. 23–4.
16 Marija Gimbutas, *The Goddesses and Gods of Old Europe: 6500– 3500 BC, Myths and Cult Images* [1974] (London, 1982), pp. 11, 135.
17 Ibid., p. 135.
18 Petzinger, email correspondence with the author, 5 December 2018; Petzinger, *First Signs*, p. 4.
19 Hoffecker, *Desolate Landscapes*, p. 2. Hoffecker posits that these ideas developed further because 'symbols were used to create new forms of organization'.
20 See Alexander Marshack, *The Roots of Civilization* (New York, 1972), pp. 109–23, for a discussion of the process of making of an object and a perception of it as signifying future time.
21 An example of the age and variety of these geometric lines can be seen in the 2014 discovery in Java of a zigzag line cut deeply into a mollusc shell that was dated to 550,000–430,000 BCE.
22 Jean Molino, 'Introduction', Henri Focillon, *The Life of Forms in Art* [1934] (New York, 1996), p. 2.
23 Denise Dreher, *From the Neck Up: An Illustrated Guide to Hatmaking* (Minneapolis, MN, 1981), pp. 7–9.
24 *Encyclopedia of Stone Age Art*, www.visual-arts-cork.com (accessed 3 February 2017). A cupule at the Auditorium Cave at Bhimbetka, Madhya Pradesh, India, dates back to 290,000–700,000 BCE.

25 John Baines, *Visual and Written Culture in Ancient Egypt* (Oxford, 2010), p. 5.

26 Ibid., p. 3.

27 Marshack, *The Roots of Civilization*, pp. 109–23.

28 Marija Gimbutas, *The Language of the Goddess* (London, 1989), pp. 29, 218.

29 Thomas Dekker, *The Pleasant Comedie of Old Fortunatus* (first printed in 1600), Act 2, Scene 1.

30 The Brothers Grimm, 'The Knapsack, the Hat and the Horn', https://sites.duke.edu.

31 J. K. Rowling, *Harry Potter and the Philosopher's Stone* (London, 1997), pp. 87–8.

32 Beverly Chico, *Hats and Headwear around The World: A Cultural Encyclopedia* (Santa Barbara, CA, 2013), p. 21.

33 *The Century Dictionary* (London, 1899).

34 Ibid.

35 Eric Partridge, *The Dictionary of Historical Slang* [1937] (London, 1988), p. 97.

36 Jane Harrison, *Themis* [1911] (London, 1989), p. 21.

37 Homer, *Iliad*, trans. A. T. Murray (London, 1945), Book 5, pp. 844–5: 'Athene put on the cap of Hades, to the end that mighty Ares [god of war] should not see her.' *Iliad*, trans. Richard Lattimore (Chicago, IL, 1951), 'put on the helm of Death'. Athene was one of the most important Greek gods, presiding over wisdom, art and reason.

38 Malcolm M. Willcock, *The Companion to the Iliad* (Chicago, IL, 1976), p. 64.

39 Harrison, *Themis*, pp. 277–9. It is not uncommon for lesser deities who appear in the pantheons during the 1st millennium BCE to have been the supernal deities, a thousand years earlier in the 2nd millennium BCE. Though their status has diminished, often their physical symbols are retained.

40 Ibid., p. 294 and pp. 277–9. Harrison cites Hermes as the latter-day version of the *Agathos Daimon*, a 'very primitive fertility spirit', and she stresses that the *Agathos Daimon* (meaning 'good spirit') represented the 'collectivity' of both kingship and community.

41 Ibid., p. xvii.

42 Deities often held symbolic objects that represented their powers. An example is the caduceus (two snakes entwined around a pole), a symbol which Hermes carried. Though the caduceus is still a familiar symbol today, the connection to its ancient origins and the deity it represented is less well known.

43 Carl Jung, *Symbols of Transformation*, trans. R.F.C. Hull [1956] (Princeton, NJ, 1990), pp. 127, 205. Each Dioscuri wore a pileus, whose curved, conical sides resembled an egg.

44 See June Schlueter, 'New Light on Dekker's Fortunati', *Medieval and Renaissance Drama in England*, XVI (2013), pp. 120–35; Michael

Haldane, 'The Translation of the Unseen Self: Fortunatus, Mercury and the Wishing-hat', *Folklore*, CXVII/2 (August 2006), pp. 171–89; Michael Haldane, 'The Date of Thomas Combe's "Fortunatus" and Its Relation to Thomas Dekker's "Old Fortunatus"', *The Modern Language Review*, CI/2 (April 2006), pp. 313–24.

45 Thomas Dekker, *The Pleasant Comedie of Old Fortunatus* (London, 1600), Act 3, Scene 1.

46 See Haldane, 'The Translation of the Unseen Self'; David McInnis, *Mind-travelling and Voyage Drama in Early Modern England* (New York, 2013).

47 Haldane, 'The Translation of the Unseen Self', pp. 173, 182, 185.

48 Ibid., p. 175. See also McInnis, *Mind-travelling and Voyage Drama*, pp. 79, 81.

49 Haldane, 'The Translation of the Unseen Self', p. 175.

50 Ibid., p. 181.

51 *Deutsche Mythologie* was a three-volume work, first published in 1835. The fourth volume was added posthumously. The English translation was published between 1882 and 1888.

52 Jacob Grimm, *Teutonic Mythology*, trans. and ed. James Steven Stallybrass, 4th edn (London 1888), vol. IV, pp. 1329–30. Volume IV is considered a 'supplement'. It contains Grimm's notes, which were accumulated after his death and added as notes or footnotes by Professor Elard Hugo Meyer in regard to the work of volumes I–III.

53 Ibid., p. 1330.

54 Haldane, 'The Translation of the Unseen Self', p. 182.

TWO

SKILL / THE HATMAKERS

1 Philip Treacy, interview with Jeanne Beker, 'Meet the Rad Hatter for the Royal Wedding', *Globe and Mail*, 18 April 2011, www.theglobeandmail.com.

2 Jane Loewen, *Millinery* (New York, 1926), p. 6.

3 Ibid., p. 19.

4 Michael Sonenscher, *The Hatters of Eighteenth-century France* (Berkeley, CA, 1987).

5 Bonnie S. Anderson and Judith P. Zinsser, *A History of Their Own: Women in Europe from Prehistory to the Present* (London, 1988), vol. I, pp. 369–72.

6 David Bensman, *The Practice of Solidarity: American Hat Finishers in the Nineteenth Century* (Urbana, IL, 1985), p. 8; Sonenscher, *The Hatters of Eighteenth-century France*, pp. 111–16.

7 Stephen Yafa, *Cotton: The Biography of a Revolutionary Fiber* (London, 2005), p. 31.

8 William Sewell and Michael Sonenscher, 'The Empire of Fashion and the Rise of Capitalism in Eighteenth-century France', *Past and*

Present, 206 (February 2010), p. 83. Sewell refers to Neil McKendrick, John Brewer and J. H. Plumb, *The Birth of a Consumer Society: The Commercialization of Eighteenth-century England* (London, 1982), and quotes McKendrick's observation that the 'consumer revolution' was as consequential as the Industrial Revolution.

9 See W. Carew Hazlitt, *The Livery Companies of the Cities of London* (London, 1892), p. 120; Jutta Zander Seidel, 'Ready-to-wear Clothing in Germany in the Sixteenth and Seventeenth Centuries: New Ready-made Garments and Second-hand Clothes Trade', in *Per una storia della moda pronta, problemi e ricerche* (A History of Ready-to-Wear: Problems and Research); proceedings of the Fifth International Conference of CISST (The Italian Center for the Study of the History of Textiles), Milan, 26–28 February 1990 (Florence, 1991), pp. 9–10.

10 See R. Broby-Johansen, *Body and Clothes: An Illustrated History of Costume* (New York, 1968), p. 126.

11 For further discussion see Anne H. Van Buren and Robert S. Wierck, *Illuminating Fashion: Dress in the Art of Medieval France and the Netherlands, 1325–1515* (New York, 2011), pp. 1–37; Ulinka Rublack and Maria Hayward, eds, *The First Fashion Book: The Book of Clothes of Matthäus and Veit Konrad Schwarz of Augsburg* (London, 2015), pp. 2–3, 12–14. This fashion consciousness, launched in the fourteenth century, spanned the Renaissance and fostered innovation in the sewing professions and support for the financial success of the textile trade. Courtly attire, well into the sixteenth century, was based on an ensemble look, relying not just on clothes but on accessories. Hats were often the most important addition. To be well dressed was thought to be cultured.

12 Seidel, 'Ready-to-wear Clothing in Germany', pp. 9–10.

13 Ibid.

14 Shane White and Graham White, *Stylin': African American Expressive Culture from its Beginnings to the Zoot Suit* (Ithaca, NY, 1998), p. 6; Juliet K. Walker, *The History of Black Business in America: Capitalism, Race, Entrepreneurship*, vol. I: *To 1865*, 2nd edn (Chapel Hill, NC, 2009), pp. 96–7.

15 Yafa, *Cotton*, p. 31.

16 Sonenscher, *The Hatters of Eighteenth-century France*, pp. 106–17.

17 See Clare Haru Crowston, *Fabricating Women: The Seamstresses of Old Regime France, 1675–1791* (Durham, NC, 2001), p. 174; Clare Haru Crowston, *Credit, Fashion, Sex: Economies of Regard in Old Regime France* (Durham, NC, 2013), p. 12.

18 Broby-Johansen, *Body and Clothes*, p. 132.

19 See Crowston, *Credit, Fashion, Sex*, p. 143; Crowston, *Fabricating Women*, p. 175.

20 The Mercer guild kept the *marchandes de monde* under the confines of Mercer guild law, which inscribed their work as 'talent' (that is,

not a learned skill, and thus only mercers and mercers' wives could practise legally). Typical of guilds at this time, the only way women could be in, or work within, the mercers' guild was as a spouse. In this way, before 1776, the Mercer guild kept the fashion merchants, most especially the women, from uniting.

21 Crowston, *Credit, Fashion, Sex*, p. 148.
22 Caroline Weber, *Queen of Fashion: What Marie Antoinette Wore to the Revolution* (New York, 2006), p. 102.
23 Crowston, *Credit, Fashion, Sex*, p. 145.
24 Weber, *Queen of Fashion*, p. 103.
25 Sewell and Sonenscher, 'Empire of Fashion', p. 87.
26 Ibid., p. 84.
27 See Elizabeth Kowaleski-Wallace, *Consuming Subjects: Women, Shopping, and Business in the Eighteenth Century* (New York, 1997).
28 Wendy Gamber, *The Female Economy: Milliners and Dressmaking Trades, 1860–1930* (Urbana, IL, 1992), p. 206. Gamber speculates that the reason for this handover (from male tailors to female milliners/dressmakers) was to do with new eighteenth-century concepts of body privacy (a man should not fit clothes on a woman) and new styles in sexually defining clothes.
29 Gamber, *The Female Economy*, p. 12.
30 Ibid., p. 206.
31 Susan Ingall Lewis, 'Beyond Horatia Alger: Breaking through Gendered Assumptions about Business "Success" in Mid-nineteenth-century America', *Business and Economic History*, XXIV/1 (Autumn 1995), p. 101.
32 Gamber, *The Female Economy*, p. 209.
33 Walker, *The History of Black Business in America*, pp. 141–2.
34 Gamber, *The Female Economy*, p. 196.
35 Ibid., p. 196.
36 Crowston, *Credit, Fashion, Sex*, p. 140.
37 Lewis, 'Beyond Horatia Alger', pp. 99–101.
38 See Wendy Gamber, 'Gendered Concerns: Thoughts on the History of Business and the History of Women', *Business and Economic History*, XXIII/1 (Autumn 1994); Lewis, 'Beyond Horatia Alger'. Gamber points out that many kinds of prosperous businesses in other categories (such as peddling) were neglected.
39 Lewis, 'Beyond Horatia Alger', p. 98. Contracts with suppliers show that its sales were continuous. Lewis shows that records reveal that in mid-nineteenth-century Albany, New York, women's entrepreneurship could thrive despite ledgers which listed negative credit opinions:

> A small business, characterized as 'worth 00' by credit examiners, might well survive for decades. Thus, the trade of milliner Ellen O'Brien was judged a 'small concern,'

'slow' and 'worse than slow,' in the years between 1859 and
1868, but her business was still listed in city directories as
late as 1895. Similarly, despite repetitive credit evaluations
such as 'small,' 'not good,' 'of no account,' 'very small,'
'no improvement,' and 'm[a]k[in]g oo over expenses,' Anna
Andrews operated a millinery establishment for twenty-five
years, eventually employing her sons as clerks.

40 See Lewis, 'Beyond Horatia Alger', pp. 97–105; Jacqueline Barbara
Carr, 'Marketing Gentility: Boston's Businesswomen, 1780–1830',
New England Quarterly, LXXXII/1 (March 2009), p. 25.

41 Lewis, 'Beyond Horatia Alger', pp. 99–101; Carr, 'Marketing
Gentility', p. 29, n. 10.

42 As an example, in 1860, in Norfolk, Virginia, one of the South's
most prosperous and important port towns, a forty-year-old white,
unmarried milliner (Mrs Butts) was worth $13,000, making her the
town's wealthiest businesswoman. She had three apprentices (female)
who also lived with her. Though women held 88 per cent of the
millinery trade pre-Civil War and then 62 per cent after, millinery
was one of the businesses that continued to bring women success
post-Civil War. By 1867, having survived the Civil War, Mrs Butts's
financial status had ranged up to $25,000, an almost unthinkable
wealth for her era.

43 Crowston, *Credit, Fashion, Sex*.

44 Weber, *Queen of Fashion*, p. 103.

45 Ibid., p. 127. Bertin was bullied by a duke when she refused him.
She wouldn't stand up in his company, though protocol required it,
and she spoke out against his abuse.

46 Will Bashor, *Marie Antoinette's Head: The Royal Hairdresser, the
Queen, and the Revolution* (Guilford, CT, 2013), p. 51.

47 Caroline Moorhead, *Dancing to the Precipice: The Life of
Lucie de la Tour du Pin, Eyewitness to an Era* (New York, 2009),
p. 65.

48 Amy Louise Erickson, 'Eleanor Mosley and Other Milliners in the
City of London Companies, 1700–1750', *History Workshop Journal*,
71 (Spring 2011), p. 150.

49 Lynn M. Alexander, 'Creating a Symbol: The Seamstress in Victorian
Literature', *Tulsa Studies in Women's Literature*, XVIII/1 (Spring
1999), p. 31. Alexander quotes E. L. Devonald, 'The Second Report
of the Children's Employment Commission', *Parliamentary Papers*,
XIV/625 (1843), footnote, p. 236.

50 Ruth Rosen, *The Lost Sisterhood: Prostitution in America, 1900–1918*
(Baltimore, MD, 1982), p. 2.

51 Georges Lefebvre, *The Great Fear of 1789: Rural Panic in
Revolutionary France* (New York, 1973), pp. 14–16. Quickly rising
prices meant that even steady workers had to resort to begging.

52 Carr, 'Marketing Gentility', p. 29. 'In addition to the hats they crafted, milliners also sold a wide variety of ornamental accessories, fabrics, and other notions to both female and male customers.'

53 Gamber, *The Female Economy,* p. 15.

54 Eric Partridge, *Penguin Dictionary of Historical Slang* (London, 1973), p. 579.

55 Ibid., p. 646.

56 Will and Ariel Durant, *The Reformation: A History of European Civilization from Wyclif to Calvin, 1300–1564* (New York, 1957), p. 469. John Calvin regarded sexual excess, prostitution (which was legal in some cities) and entertainments such as dancing as so immoral, he construed them as 'treason against God'. See also Ulinka Rublack and Maria Hayward, eds, *The First Fashion Book: The Books of Clothes of Matthäus and Veit Konrad Schwarz of Augsburg* (London, 2015), p. 14.

57 Peter Linebaugh, *Ned Ludd and Queen Mab: Machine-breaking, Romanticism, and the Several Commons of 1811–12* (New York, 2016), pp. 12–13. Linebaugh suggests that the enclosure laws, which appropriated public land for private use, were not only taking literal property but were enacting enclosures in the cultural mindset. Linebaugh argues that the enclosure mindset appeared in the new phenomenon of extensive prison building, enclosure of the rivers and ports with canal locks and high docks, the centralization of a permanent military presence in barrack buildings, suppression of the press, and the walling-off of private and public spaces according to gender affiliations.

58 Timothy Gilfoyle, *City of Eros: New York City, Prostitution and the Commercialization of Sex, 1790–1920* (New York, 1992), p. 61. Gilfoyle notes that 'in the popular imagination, milliners and servants were frequently equated with lax sexual morals, if not prostitution.' The *Weekly Rake*, for example, claimed milliners' shops contained 'pretty women . . . intrigues, love matches, seductions, and many other things'.

59 Hollis Clayson, *Painted Love: Prostitution in the French Art of the Impressionist Era* (Los Angeles, CA, 2003), p. 113. Clayson quotes C. J. Lecour, *La Prostitution à Paris et à Londres* (Paris, 1872).

60 Lujo Basserman, *The Oldest Profession: A History of Prostitution* [1965] (New York 1993), p. 226.

61 Émile Zola, *The Ladies' Paradise* [1883], trans. Brian Nelson (Oxford, 1993), pp. 234–6.

62 Simon Kelly, '"Silk and Feather, Satin and Straw": Degas, Women, and the Paris Millinery Trade', in *Degas, Impressionism, and the Paris Millinery Trade*, ed. Simon Kelly and Esther Bell (San Francisco, CA, and Munich, 2017), pp. 17–49.

63 Clayson, *Painted Love*, p. 121. Clayson cites painters Edgar Degas, Eva Gonzalès, Pierre-Auguste Renoir and Édouard Manet as being especially attracted to the subject, and cites their work regarding millinery as falling between 1877 and 1885. Degas chose this subject repeatedly between 1882 and 1885.

Blow, Detmar, and Tom Sykes, *Blow by Blow: The Story of Isabella Blow* (London, 2010)

Blume, Mary, *The Master of Us All: Balenciaga, His Workrooms, His World* (New York, 2013)

Broby-Johansen, R., *Body and Clothes: An Illustrated History of Costume* (New York, 1968)

Brook, Timothy, *Vermeer's Hat: The Seventeenth Century and the Dawn of the Global World* (London, 2008)

Brooks, John, ed., *The 1977 South American Handbook* (Bath, 1976)

Bruce, Robert V., *1877: Year of Violence* [1958] (Chicago, IL, 1989)

Calefato, Patrizia, trans. Lisa Adams, *The Clothed Body* (New York, 2006)

Cameron, Averil, and Amelie Kurht, *Images of Women in Antiquity* (Detroit, MI, 1983)

Carr, Jacqueline Barbara, 'Marketing Gentility: Boston's Businesswomen, 1780–1830', *The New England Quarterly*, LXXXII/1 (March 2009)

The Century Dictionary [1899] (London 1904)

Chang, Ting, 'Hats and Hierarchy in Gustave Courbet's "The Meeting"', *The Art Bulletin*, LXXXVI/4 (December 2004)

Chico, Beverly, *Hats and Headwear around The World: A Cultural Encyclopedia* (Santa Barbara, CA, 2013)

Chude-Sokei, Louis, *The Last 'Darky': Bert Williams, Black-on-Black Minstrelsy, and the African Diaspora* (Durham, NC, 2006)

Clark, Fiona, *Hats* [1982] (New York, 1988)

Clayson, Hollis, *Painted Love: Prostitution in the French Art of the Impressionist Era* (Los Angeles, CA, 2003)

Cockrell, Dale, *Demons of Disorder: Early Blackface Minstrels and Their World* (New York, 1997)

Crane, Diane, *Fashion and Its Social Agendas: Class, Gender, and Identity in Clothing* (Chicago, IL, 2000)

Crowston, Clare Haru, *Fabricating Women: The Seamstresses of Old Regime France, 1675–1791* (Durham, NC, 2001)

——, *Credit, Fashion, Sex: Economies of Regard in Old Regime France* (Durham, NC, 2013)

Cuthbertson, Bennett, *A System for the Compleat Interior Management and Economy of a Battalion of Infantry* (Dublin, 1768)

Daché, Lilly, *Talking through My Hats* (London, 1956)

David, Alison Matthews, *Fashion Victims: The Dangers of Dress Past and Present* (Durham, NC, 2006)

Davidson, Nicholas, 'Theology, Nature and the Law: Sexual Sin and Sexual Crime in Italy from the 14th to the 17th Century', in *Crime, Society and the Law in Renaissance Italy*, ed. Trevor Dean and K.J.P. Lowe (New York, 1994)

de Marly, Diana, *Dress in North America: The New World, 1492–1800*, vol. 1 (New York, 1990)

Dekker, Thomas, *The Pleasant Comedie of Old Fortunatus* (London, 1600)

Dreher, Denise, *From the Neck Up: An Illustrated Guide to Hatmaking* (New York, 1981)

Durant, Will and Ariel, *The Reformation: A History of European Civilization from Wyclif to Calvin, 1300–1564* (New York, 1957)

Duras, Marguerite, *The Lover* (New York, 1998)

Earshaw, Pat, *Lace in Fashion: From the Sixteenth to Twentieth Centuries* (Guilford, CT, 1985)

Erickson, Amy Louise, 'Eleanor Mosley and Other Milliners in the City of London Companies, 1700–1750', *History Workshop Journal*, 71 (Spring 2011)

Evans, Caroline, *The Mechanical Smile: Modernism and the First Fashion Shows in France and America, 1900–1929* (New Haven, CT, 2013)

Ewing, Elizabeth, *Fur in Dress* (North Pomfret, VT, 1981)

Farnsworth, Marjorie, *The Ziegfeld Follies: A History in Text and Pictures* (London, 1956)

Ferrari, Mary, '"Obliged to Earn Subsistence for Themselves": Women Artisans in Charleston, South Carolina, 1763–1808', *South Carolina Historical Magazine*, CVI/4 (October 2005)

Fife, Graeme, *The Terror: The Shadow of the Guillotine: France, 1792–1794* (London, 2004)

Foner, Philip S., *The Fur and Leather Workers Union: A Story of Dramatic Struggles and Achievements* (Newark, NJ, 1950)

——, *The Great Labor Uprising of 1877* (New York, 1977)

Foster, Helen Bradley, '*New Raiments of Self*': African American Clothing in the Antebellum South* (Oxford, 1997)

Frisa, Maria Luisa, ed., *Excess: Fashion and the Underground in the '80s* (Milan, 2004)

Furgurson, Ernest B., 'The Man Who Shot the Man Who Shot Lincoln: The Hatter Boston Corbett Was Celebrated as a Hero For Killing John Wilkes Booth', *American Scholar*, LXXVIII/2 (Spring 2009)

Gamber, Wendy, *The Female Economy: Milliners and Dressmaking Trades, 1860–1930* (Urbana, IL, 1992)

——, 'Gendered Concerns: Thoughts on the History of Business and the History of Women', *Business and Economic History*, XXIII/1 (Autumn 1994), pp. 129–40

Gay, Peter, *Style in History* (New York, 1974)

Gebauer, Paul, *Art of Cameroon* (New York, 1979)

Gilfoyle, Timothy, *City of Eros: New York City, Prostitution and the Commercialization of Sex, 1790–1920* (New York, 1992)

Gimbutas, Marija, *The Goddesses and Gods of Old Europe, 6500–3500 BC: Myths and Cult Images* [1974] (London, 1982)

——, *The Language of the Goddess* (London, 1989)

Ginsburg, Madeleine, *The Hat: Trends and Traditions* (Hauppauge, NY, 1990)

Glynn, Prudence, *In Fashion: Dress in the Twentieth Century* (New York, 1978)

Godwin, Godfrey, *The Private World of Ottoman Women* (London, 2006)

Sparks, Edith, *Capital Intentions: Female Proprietors in San Francisco, 1850–1920* (Chapel Hill, NC, 2006)

Stansell, Christine, *City of Women: Sex and Class in New York, 1789–1860* (New York, 1986)

Steinberg, Neil, *Hatless Jack* (New York, 2004)

Styles, John, *The Dress of the People: Everyday Fashion in Eighteenth-century England* (New Haven, CT, 2007)

Svoboda, Josef, *The Secret of Theatrical Space*, trans. and ed. M. Burian (New York, 2000)

Tarlo, Emma, *Visibly Muslim: Fashion, Politics, Faith* (New York, 2010)

Thaarup, Aage, *Heads and Tales* (London, 1956)

Tonna, Charlotte Elizabeth, *The Wrongs of Women: Milliners and Dressmakers* (New York, 1844)

Van Buren, Anne H., and Robert S. Wierck, *Illuminating Fashion: Dress in the Art of Medieval France and the Netherlands, 1325–1515* (New York, 2011)

Van Kleeck, Mary, *Artificial Flower Makers* (New York, 1913)

——, *A Seasonal Industry: A Study of the Millinery Trade in New York* (New York, 1917)

Von Petzinger, Genevieve, *The First Signs: Unlocking the Mysteries of the World's Oldest Symbols* (New York, 2016)

Walker, Juliet K., *The History of Black Business in America: Capitalism, Race, Entrepreneurship*, vol. I: *To 1865*, 2nd edn (Chapel Hill, NC, 2009)

Weber, Caroline, *Queen of Fashion: What Marie Antoinette Wore to the Revolution* (New York, 2006)

Weissman, Jenna Joselit, *A Perfect Fit: Clothes, Character and the Promise of America* (New York, 2001)

White, Shane, and Graham White, *Stylin': African American Expressive Culture from Its Beginnings to the Zoot Suit* (Ithaca, NY, 1999)

Wilcox, R. Turner, *The Mode in Hats and Headdress* (New York, 1945)

Willcock, Malcolm M., *The Companion to the Iliad* (Chicago, IL, 1976)

Williams, Haydn, *Turquerie: An Eighteenth-century European Fantasy* (London, 2014)

Winter, William, *The Life of David Belasco* (New York, 1918)

Wollen, Peter, 'Out of the Past', in *Raiding the Icebox* (Bloomington, IN, 1993)

Woods, Caroline H., *The Diary of a Milliner* (New York, 1867)

Yafa, Stephen, *Cotton: The Biography of a Revolutionary Fiber* (London, 2005)

Zola, Émile, *Au Bonheur des dames (The Ladies' Paradise)* [1883], trans. Brian Nelson (Oxford, 1993)

ACKNOWLEDGEMENTS

For their ideas, enthusiasm, skills and research that have bolstered this book I happily thank Leslie Dick, Alex Westhalle and Dave Bermingham. I thank, also, the people at Reaktion Books: Michael Leaman for his support of this project over a number of years, and Susannah Jayes, Aimee Selby and Martha Jay for their unwavering help in putting the book together. Thanks, also, to all the writers whose fascinating work broadened my mind as I researched this book.

PHOTO ACKNOWLEDGEMENTS

The author and publishers wish to express their thanks to the below sources of illustrative material and/or permission to reproduce it.

AKG Images: pp. 14 (Erich Lessing), 35 (Pictures from History); Alamy: pp. 11 top (Chronicle), 15 (Aurelian Images), 17 (imageBROKER), 29 (Heritage Image Partnership Ltd), 44 (PRISMA ARCHIVO), 52 (Neil Baylis), 54 (Granger Historical Picture Archive), 55 (INTERFOTO), 58 (ART Collection), 71 (Granger Historial Picture Archive), 88 (First Collection), 94 (Heritage Image Partnership), 97 (World History Archive), 98 (Granger Historical Picture Archive), 115 (Age Fotostock), 116 (Luciano de Polo Stokkete), 119 (Artokoloro Quint Lox Limited), 124 (Azoor Photo Collection), 125 (Berengere Cavalier), 131 (Arterra Picture Library), 145 (Vintage Images), 150 (Chronicle), 153 (Randy Duchaine), 160 (Chronicle), 171 (World History Archive), 177 (INTER-FOTO), 180 (Archive Farms Inc), 181 (Everett Collection Inc), 184 (Artepics/© ADAGP, Paris and DACS, London 2019), 186 (cineclassico), p. 205 (Panther Media Gmbh); Dinu Bodiciu: p. 202 (Photography Christopher Agius Burke); Bridgeman Images: p. 13 (Pitt Rivers Museum, Oxford, UK); Condé Nast: p. 185 (© The Estate of Edward Steichen/ARS, NY and DACS, London 2019); Harvard Theatre Collection, Houghton Library, Harvard University: p. 135 (TS 939.5.3); Herzog August Library, Wolfenbüttel: p. 47; Don Hitchcock: p. 30; Getty Images: pp. 10 bottom (Bertrand Langlois), 18 (JIJI PRESS/AFP), 77 (Hulton Archive), 82 (Photo by Time Life Pictures/The LIFE Picture Collection), 120 (Duncan1890), 138 (Photo by © Hulton-Deutsch Collection/CORBIS), 163 (Frennie Shivambu/Gallo Images), 175 (Popperfoto), 179 (General Photographic Agency), 188 (Alfred Eisenstaedt/ullstein bild), 196 (Kevin Mazur/Wireimage); Iconic Images: p. 191 (Norman Parkinson); iStockphoto: p. 8 (AlexanderFagundes); Library of Congress, Washington DC: pp. 107, 129, 170; Mary Evans Picture Library: pp. 158 (Spaarnestad Photo Collection/Wiel van der Randen), 174 (© Galliera/Roger-Viollet), 195 (Illustrated London News Ltd); Christine Mathieu: p. 159 (Museum of Art and History of Granville-France); The Metropolitan Museum of Art, New York: pp. 45, 79, 178; The Morgan Library & Museum, New York: p. 157 (MS M.638, fol. 43v. Purchased by J. P. Morgan); Museum of Applied Arts and Sciences, Sydney: p. 189;